INSIDE THE MINDS

Environmental Law Enforcement and Compliance

Leading Lawyers on Communicating with Enforcement Agencies, Overcoming Compliance Challenges, and Developing Response Strategies

ASPATORE

Inside the Minds Project Manager, Ryann Burnett; edited by Michaela Falls; proofread by Melanie Zimmerman

ISBN 978-0-314-27845-6

For corrections, updates, comments or any other inquiries please e-mail TLR.AspatoreEditorial@thomson.com.

First Printing, 2011
10 9 8 7 6 5 4 3 2 1

Mat #41201130

Praise for *Inside the Minds*

"This series provides a practical and focused discussion of the leading issues in law today." – John V. Biernacki, Partner, Jones Day

"*Inside the Minds* draws from the collective experience of the best professionals. The books are informative from an academic, and, more importantly, practical perspective. I highly recommend them." – Keith M. Aurzada, Partner, Bryan Cave LLP

"Aspatore's *Inside the Minds* series provides practical, cutting edge advice from those with insight into the real world challenges that confront businesses in the global economy." – Michael Bednarek, Partner, Shearman & Sterling LLP

"What to read when you want to be in the know—topical, current, practical, and useful information on areas of the law that everyone is talking about." – Erika L. Morabito, Partner, Patton Boggs LLP

"Some of the best insight around from sources in the know" – Donald R. Kirk, Shareholder, Fowler White Boggs PA

"The *Inside the Minds* series provides a unique window into the strategic thinking of key players in business and law." – John M. Sylvester, Partner, K&L Gates LLP

"Comprehensive analysis and strategies you won't find anywhere else." – Stephen C. Stapleton, Of Counsel, Dykema Gossett PLLC

"The *Inside the Minds* series is a real hands-on, practical resource for cutting edge issues." – Trey Monsour, Partner, Haynes and Boone LLP

"A tremendous resource, amalgamating commentary from leading professionals that is presented in a concise, easy to read format." – Alan H. Aronson, Shareholder, Akerman Senterfitt

"Unique and invaluable opportunity to gain insight into the minds of experienced professionals." – Jura C. Zibas, Partner, Lewis Brisbois Bisgaard & Smith LLP

"A refreshing collection of strategic insights, not dreary commonplaces, from some of the best of the profession." – Roger J. Magnuson, Partner, Dorsey & Whitney LLP

"Provides valuable insights by experienced practitioners into practical and theoretical developments in today's ever-changing legal world." – Elizabeth Gray, Partner, Willkie, Farr & Gallagher LLP

"This series provides invaluable insight into the practical experiences of lawyers in the trenches." – Thomas H. Christopher, Partner, Kilpatrick Stockton LLP

ASPATORE

Aspatore Books, a Thomson Reuters business, exclusively publishes C-Level executives and partners from the world's most respected companies and law firms. Each publication provides professionals of all levels with proven business and legal intelligence from industry insiders—direct and unfiltered insight from those who know it best. Aspatore Books is committed to publishing an innovative line of business and legal titles that lay forth principles and offer insights that can have a direct financial impact on the reader's business objectives.

Each chapter in the *Inside the Minds* series offers thought leadership and expert analysis on an industry, profession, or topic, providing a future-oriented perspective and proven strategies for success. Each author has been selected based on their experience and C-Level standing within the business and legal communities. *Inside the Minds* was conceived to give a first-hand look into the leading minds of top business executives and lawyers worldwide, presenting an unprecedented collection of views on various industries and professions.

CONTENTS

Understanding Environmental Law Enforcement

Karl R. Heisler

Partner

Katten Muchin Rosenman LLP

ASPATORE

The Role of Enforcement in Environmental Law

Empirical evidence has demonstrated that civil and criminal enforcement has deterred violations and enhanced environmental protection.[1] Enforcement has increased the likelihood that offenders will suffer imprisonment, material financial liabilities, injunctive relief, reputational losses, heightened governmental scrutiny, and decreased stock value. Enforcement has also increased the likelihood that non-offenders will promote organizational cultures that encourage environmental stewardship and will pursue state-of-the-art environmental management systems beyond what is required by the letter of the law.

Air, water, and land are the world's three most valuable resources, and without the threat of enforcement, voluntary cooperation among those sharing and using these resources has, over time, proved woefully insufficient. This, as Garrett Harden wrote in 1968, is the result of the "tragedy of the commons," a dilemma that surfaces when those acting in their own self-interests destroy finite resources shared by all:

> [T]he tragedy of the commons reappears in problems of pollution. Here it is not a question of taking something out of the commons, but of putting something in – sewage, or chemical, radioactive, and heat wastes into water; noxious and dangerous fumes into the air, and distracting and unpleasant advertising signs into the line of sight. The calculations of utility are much the same as before. The rational man finds that his share of the cost of the wastes he discharges into the commons is less than the cost of purifying his wastes before releasing them. Since this is true for everyone, we are locked into a system of "fouling our own nest," so long as we behave only as independent, rational, free-enterprisers.[2]

---

[1] *See, e.g.*, Carol E. Dinkins et al., *The Role of Public and Private Litigants in Promoting Environmental Corporate Social Responsibility*, 21 FORDHAM ENVTL. L. REV. 123 (2010); Jonathan Karpoff et al., *The Reputational Penalties for Environmental Violations: Empirical Evidence*, 48 J.L. & ECON. 653 (2005); Mark A. Cohen, *Empirical Research on the Deterrent Effect of Environmental Monitoring and Enforcement*, 30 Envtl. L. Rep. (Envtl. Law Inst.) 10,245 (2000).

[2] Garrett Hardin, *The Tragedy of the Commons*, SCIENCE, Dec. 13, 1968, at 1243-48.

The Clean Air Act, the Clean Water Act, the Comprehensive Environmental Response and Compensation Act (CERCLA), and the Federal Insecticide, Fungicide, and Rodenticide Act (FIFRA), among other environmental regimes, were legislative responses to protect the commons, and each was inspired by its own tragedy or set of tragedies:

- The Clean Air Act: In 1948, a thick cloud of air pollution formed above the industrial town of Donora, Pennsylvania, killing twenty people and causing sickness in 6,000 others.[3] In 1952, more than 3,000 people died in what became known as London's "Killer Fog."[4] In 1984, a chemical disaster in Bhopal, India killed thousands.[5]
- The Clean Water Act: The Cuyahoga River in Cleveland, Ohio repeatedly caught fire over the span of one hundred years due to excess industrial pollution.[6] In the 1960s, Lake Erie supported algae blooms over the entire portion of the western basin due to excess municipal, industrial, and agricultural runoff.[7] During the same period, the Hudson River contained bacteria levels 170 times the safe limit.[8]
- CERCLA: In perhaps the most notorious environmental incident in the nation's history, the City of Niagara Falls Board of Education purchased a toxic waste dump from Hooker Chemical in 1953, then constructed a public elementary school and a children's playground on the property.[9] Years later, toxic waste

[3] *Understanding the Clean Air Act*, EPA.GOV, http://www.epa.gov/air/peg/understand.html (last visited July 6, 2011).
[4] *Id.*
[5] *Reducing Toxic Air Pollutants*, EPA.GOV, http://www.epa.gov/air/peg/toxics.html (last visited July 6, 2011).
[6] *Cuyahoga River Fire*, OHIOHISTORYCENTRAL.ORG, http://www.ohiohistorycentral.org/entry.php?rec=1642 (last visited July 6, 2011).
[7] *Detroit River-Western Lake Erie Basin Indicator Project*, EPA.GOV, http://www.epa.gov/med/grosseile_site/indicators/algae-blooms.html (last visited July 6, 2011).
[8] Carol M. Browner, Administrator, U.S. Environmental Protection Agency, Remarks Prepared for Delivery at the 25th Anniversary of the Clean Water Act (Oct. 17, 1997), http://yosemite.epa.gov/opa/admpress.nsf/a162fa4bfc0fd2ef8525701a004f20d7/872d86a1679743df8525701a0052e3a5!OpenDocument&Highlight=0
[9] *Love Canal: A Special Report to the Governor & Legislature: April 1981*, NY.GOV, http://www.health.state.ny.us/environmental/investigations/love_canal/lcreport.htm (last visited July 6, 2011).

from the "Love Canal" neighborhood was reported to have seeped into school yards and puddled in basements.[10] Hundreds of families were evaluated.[11]

- FIFRA: In 1962, Rachel Carson published *Silent Spring*, writing of pesticide use in California that could "provide a lethal dose for five to ten times the whole world's population."[12] In the wake of unprecedented public reaction, Congress responded soon thereafter with significant enhancements to FIFRA. Carson's work is also widely credited with spurring the grassroots movement that ultimately led to the creation of the US Environmental Protection Agency (EPA).

Because of decades of civil and criminal enforcement efforts, there have been marked improvements. On its fortieth anniversary, the EPA announced that the number of Americans receiving water that meets health standards has increased by as much as 13 percent in approximately the last twenty years.[13] The EPA announced that total emissions of the six principal air pollutants have decreased by more than 41 percent over the same period.[14] EPA administrator Lisa Jackson recently announced that, over the last forty years, the air is 60 percent cleaner while the nation's gross domestic product is up 207 percent.[15] In 2010, federal enforcement efforts contributed to commitments to reduce, treat, or eliminate over 1.4 billion pounds of air, water, and land pollution; to properly treat an estimated 11.8 billion pounds of hazardous waste; to invest an estimated $8 billion in pollution control and environmental improvement projects that will improve water quality; and to invest an estimated $12 billion on pollution controls and environmental projects to clean up communities.[16] Although

---

[10] *The Love Canal Tragedy*, EPA.GOV, http://www.epa.gov/history/topics/lovecanal/01.html (last visited July 6, 2011).

[11] Anthony DePalma, *Love Canal Declared Clean, Ending Toxic Horror*, NYTimes.com (March 18, 2004), http://www.nytimes.com/2004/03/18/nyregion/love-canal-declared-clean-ending-toxic-horror.html

[12] RACHEL CARSON, SILENT SPRING (1962).

[13] *40 Years of Achievements, 1970-2010*, EPA.GOV, http://www.epa.gov/40th/achieve.html (last visited July 6, 2011).

[14] *40th Anniversary of the Clean Air Act*, EPA.GOV, http://www.epa.gov/oar/caa/40th.html (last visited July 6, 2011).

[15] Interview with Lisa Jackson, Administrator, EPA, *The Daily Show with Jon Stewart*, May 19, 2011.

[16] *Compliance and Enforcement Annual Results 2010 Fiscal Year*, EPA.GOV, http://www.epa.gov/compliance/resources/reports/endofyear/eoy2010/index.html (last

how these pollution benefits, or "beans," are counted is more of an art than a science, these are noteworthy reductions.

Yet, much work remains. Acid rain, climate change, ozone depletion, and toxic air pollutants pose significant threats to human health and the environment. Millions of Americans live in areas with air pollution levels that persistently exceed national ambient air quality standards. Non-point source runoff, stormwater management, and aging municipal drinking and wastewater infrastructure present serious enforcement challenges. As many as 8 percent of Americans do not receive water that meets health standards. By some accounts, beach closings, red tides, dead zones, nutrient pollution, and sewage pollution are still on the rise.[17] Catastrophic environmental incidents continue to occur. On April 20, 2010, the Deepwater Horizon drilling rig exploded in the Gulf of Mexico, off the coast of Louisiana, killing eleven men and injuring seventeen others.[18] Oil flowed freely into the Gulf for nearly three months, making it the largest accidental oil spill in history.[19]

A Note on Deterrence and Environmental Economics

Enforcement has been, and will continue to be, predicated on the theory of deterrence—the inhibition of illicit human and corporate behavior by fear of punishment. As Cesare Beccaria wrote in *An Essay on Crimes and Punishments* in 1794:

> It is better to prevent crimes than to punish them. This is the fundamental principle of good legislation, which is the art of conducting men to the *maximum* of happiness, and

visited July 6, 2011).

[17] *The 35th Anniversary of the Clean Water Act: Successes and Future Challenges: Hearing Before the H. Comm. on Transp. and Infrastructure*, 110th Cong. (2007) (testimony of Peter Lehner, Executive Director, Natural Resources Defense Council).

[18] National Commission on the BP Deepwater Horizon Oil Spill and Offshore Drilling, Report to the President, DEEP WATER: THE GULF OIL DISASTER AND THE FUTURE OF OFFSHORE DRILLING (January 2011) http://www.oilspillcommission.gov/sites/default/files/documents/DEEPWATER_ReporttothePresident_FINAL.pdf.

[19] *Id.*

> to the *minimum* of misery, if we may apply this mathematical expression to the good and evil of life.[20]

Economists, however, differ on how to achieve the goal of deterrence (i.e., the extent to which increases in enforcement outweigh the benefits of compliance). Hundreds of articles have been written espousing various versions of economic theory as support for enforcement policies. In 1968, Gary Becker published one of the more renowned and oft-cited economic approaches to enforcement.[21] Observing that "obedience to law is not taken for granted," he started with the base assumption that a person commits a violation if the expected utility to him exceeds the utility he could get by using his time at other activities. Taking into consideration other relevant parameters and social policy concerns, Becker, like Beccaria before him, found that enforcement should conform to a series of rational principles. For Becker, the answer was more formulaic than philosophical. He opined that effective deterrence is a function of the responses of offenders to changes in enforcement; the probability of apprehension and conviction; and the public resources available to enforce the law.

In keeping with the Becker model, the government has issued a series of environmental enforcement response and penalty policies designed to ensure that the benefits of noncompliance are outweighed by the penalties.[22] These policies take into consideration the gravity of the violation, economic benefit, potential for harm to the environment or to the regulatory program, extent of deviation from regulatory requirements, history of noncompliance, and good faith efforts (or lack thereof) to comply.

Enforcement of environmental laws, in particular, has an array of other complicating (and interesting) factors. How do we balance the "supply" of environmental violations with the "demand" for justice, given limited resources? How do we assess the severity of any given violation against the environmental performance we would expect for that particular entity or

---

[20] CESARE BECCARIA, AN ESSAY ON CRIMES AND PUNISHMENT (1794).

[21] Gary S. Becker, *Crime and Punishment: An Economic Approach*, 76 J. POL. ECON. 169, (1968).

[22] *See, e.g.*, EPA, RCRA Civil Penalty Policy (June 2003); EPA, FIFRA Enforcement Response Policy (Dec. 2009).

industry? Which violations are acceptable, and which are not? Which offenders should be punished, and which should not? How do we measure the benefits of environmental enforcement (i.e., how do we count the "beans")? To what extent should we punish entities that self-report or voluntarily disclose violations? These issues remain, and will remain, the subject of much debate.

Agencies Involved in Environmental Enforcement Cases

Most environmental enforcement efforts are led by state and local governments. Congress expressly allowed the EPA to "delegate" the authority to administer and enforce certain federal environmental statutes provided the states adopted environmental controls that were at least as stringent as federal environmental controls. In light of the varying nature of state and local enforcement regimes, this chapter focuses on federal enforcement, with an emphasis on business organizations. The role of state and local governments, as well as tribes, however, should not be overlooked.

The EPA is the lead federal environmental enforcement agency, and its resources are limited. The EPA administers programs that affect well over 300 million Americans with a staff of approximately 18,000 people, only a fraction of which are in enforcement branches.

The EPA's Office of Enforcement and Compliance Assurance (OECA) works with the ten EPA regional offices, and partners with state and tribal authorities to enforce the nation's environmental laws. The Office of Civil Enforcement (OCE) and the Office of Criminal Enforcement, Forensics, and Training (OCEFT) operate under OECA's umbrella:

- OCE is authorized to directly enforce federal civil environmental laws, but typically does so only in situations where the EPA has not delegated enforcement authority to the states, or in the event that state enforcement efforts prove inadequate (a concept known as "over-filing"). Federal civil enforcement is delegated to most states under much of the Clean Air Act, Clean Water Act, and the Resource Conservation and Recovery Act (RCRA). Regional

Counsel provide legal support to the local EPA compliance officers and serve as the local liaison to OCE.

- Conversely, OCEFT has the primary responsibility to investigate and enforce federal criminal environmental law. Federal criminal enforcement is not delegated to states. The EPA's Criminal Investigation Division (EPA CID) and the National Enforcement Investigations Center (NEIC) are the two key investigative divisions within OCEFT. Regional Criminal Enforcement Counsel provide legal support to the local EPA CID agents and serve as the local liaison to OCEFT.

Federal civil environmental enforcement matters are either brought administratively by the EPA or judicially by the US Department of Justice (DOJ), which depends on the EPA's statutory enforcement authority. Although most enforcement actions are brought administratively, the more significant cases are brought in a judicial forum. If the case is brought administratively, then the EPA can represent itself and the DOJ has no involvement. If the case is brought judicially, then the EPA must "refer" the matter to the DOJ, who then represents the EPA. Civil judicial actions involving the EPA are subject to a 1977 Memorandum of Understanding between the DOJ and the EPA, in which the DOJ retains control over the litigation, with scientific and technical support provided by the EPA.[23] The DOJ's Environment and Natural Resources Division (ENRD) has primacy over civil judicial enforcement matters, working through either the ENRD Environmental Enforcement Section or the ENRD Environmental Defense Section, depending upon the substantive nature of the enforcement action. The ENRD often brings joint civil enforcement actions with states.

Federal criminal environmental enforcement matters must all be brought by the DOJ. US Attorneys' Offices have primacy (except in rare cases), but often work closely with specialized prosecutors in the ENRD Environmental Crimes Section (ECS). Since its inception in 1982, the ENRD ECS has been instrumental in the investigation and prosecution of environmental crimes.

[23] Memorandum of Understanding Between Department of Justice and Environmental Protection Agency, 42 Fed. Reg. 48,942 (Sept. 26, 1977).

A host of other agencies participate in environmental enforcement cases, including, but not limited to, the US Fish and Wildlife Service, the Occupational Safety and Health Administration (OSHA), the US Coast Guard, the Federal Bureau of Investigation, the National Park Service, the US Forest Service, the Mine Safety and Health Administration, the Bureau of Land Management, the US Army Corps of Engineers, and the US Customs Service. By way of example, the government's response to the Deepwater Horizon explosion involved the EPA, the DOJ, the US Fish and Wildlife Service, OSHA, the National Oceanic and Atmospheric Administration, the US Department of Interior (including the National Park Service), the US Department of Homeland Security (including the US Coast Guard), the US Department of Defense, the National Institute for Public Safety and Health, and the Bureau of Ocean Energy Management, Regulation, and Enforcement.[24]

Investigative and Prosecutorial Discretion in Environmental Law Enforcement

The government has very broad discretion to investigate and prosecute environmental violations. Although certain government policies purport to control the exercise of this discretion, investigators and prosecutors have remarkable latitude in determining whether to initiate an investigation or to pursue a formal enforcement action. Environmental laws are designed to protect and improve the nation's most vital resources that surround us. They extend to the air we breathe, the water we drink, the land we love, and to just about anyone and everything that could compromise them. Environmental laws govern with an interlocking and dizzying network of federal and state statutes, regulations, ordinances, case law, and guidance. Clean Air Act regulations, for example, comprise eighteen volumes of the Code of Federal Regulations. As one commentator put it, the platform upon which to base any given regulatory investigation can thus seem boundless:

> At the field level, inspectors, auditors, and enforcement officers hold considerable power to do good and evil, to

---

[24] *Deepwater BP Oil Spill*, WHITEHOUSE.GOV, http://www.whitehouse.gov/deepwater-bp-oil-spill/ (last visited July 6, 2011).

> dispense justice or injustice. . . . The enforcement myth, which has so often saved regulators from having to account for their uses of discretion, is that they enforce the law uniformly, across the board, without fear or favor. It is not, and was never, true. They choose not to enforce laws for many reasons, some good, some bad: they did not have time; they were on their way to something more important; there were too many violators and no sensible way of choosing between them; it was a silly law; making the arrest would have provoked a riot; the offender had political connections, or was a friend, or worked for the IRS, or had a sticker on his car acknowledging contributions to a police charity.[25]

Effective enforcement, however, must be predicated on the fair and equitable treatment of the regulated community, notwithstanding the broad discretion afforded to individual investigators and prosecutors. Without an even playing field, the regulated community will not perceive the government as a rational actor, and efforts to achieve the goal of deterrence would invariability be frustrated.

The EPA has endeavored to level the playing field, albeit to varying degrees of success. In 2006, the US Government Accountability Office (GAO) released the results of a study of the EPA's enforcement activities, with an emphasis on the EPA's "Efforts to Improve and Make More Consistent Its Enforcement Activities."[26] The GAO found that there were a number of factors contributing to regional variations in environmental enforcement, including differences in philosophical approaches to enforcement, incomplete and inaccurate national enforcement data, and an inadequate workforce planning and allocation system. The GAO also found that the EPA had initiated several promising actions to address these regional variations. The EPA, for example, recently implemented a State Review

[25] Malcolm K. Sparrow, *The Regulatory Craft* (2000).

[26] U.S. GOV'T ACCOUNTABILITY OFFICE, GAO-06-840T, ENVIRONMENTAL COMPLIANCE AND ENFORCEMENT – EPA'S EFFORT TO IMPROVE AND MAKE MORE CONSISTENT ITS COMPLIANCE AND ENFORCEMENT ACTIVITIES (2006) (statement of John B. Stephenson, Director, Natural Resources and Environment, before the U.S. Senate Committee on Environment and Public Works).

Framework, in which regional and state enforcement reviews are conducted on a four-year cycle, and enforcement inconsistencies that are identified are addressed in federal grant agreements.[27] Although the EPA has made progress with respect to compiling meaningful enforcement data, the GAO found that the agency still focuses on "outputs rather than results" (i.e., on the number of facilities inspected as opposed to the actual environmental outcomes resulting from those inspections).[28] Finally, the GAO reported that the EPA had taken steps to improve management of its human capital, but that it had failed to "comprehensively assess its workforce" such that the EPA could more readily identify how many employees are needed, what technical skills are required, and how best to allocate employees across regional offices.

Given the higher stakes in criminal matters, both EPA OCEFT and the DOJ have also attempted to level the playing field by issuing internal directives to control the exercise of investigative and prosecutorial discretion.

The EPA has issued guidance on the exercise of investigative discretion in criminal case selection.[29] Issued in 1994, this guidance remains in force today. Earl Devaney, then director of the Office of Criminal Enforcement (now, OCEFT), issued a memorandum to all employees working in or in support of the criminal enforcement program that outlined "specific factors that distinguish cases meriting criminal investigation from those more appropriately pursued under civil or administrative authorities." The Devaney memo acknowledged the possibility that OCEFT would never "be large enough in size to fully defeat the ever-expanding universe of environmental crime" and sought to advance the EPA's goals through discerning case selection. This memorandum provides that case selection should be determined by the presence of (a) significant environmental harm

---

[27] State Review Framework, EPA.GOV, http://www.epa.gov/oecaerth/state/srf/index.html (last visited July 6, 2011).

[28] Notably, Steve Solow, a former Chief of Environmental Crimes at DOJ, has called for the establishment of a "Bureau of Environmental Statistics" as an independent national statistical agency. *See, e.g.*, Steve Solow & Anne Carpenter, *The State of Environmental Crime Enforcement: A Survey of Developments in 2009*, 41 Env't Rep. (BNA) 574 (Mar. 12, 2010).

[29] Memorandum from Earl E. Devaney, Director, EPA Office of Criminal Enforcement, to All Employees Working in or in Support of the Criminal Enforcement Program (Jan. 12, 1994) (regarding The Exercise of Investigative Discretion).

and (b) culpable conduct. Significant environmental harm is broadly construed to include the threat of significant harm to human health or the environment. Culpable conduct is a function of the history of repeated violations; deliberate misconduct resulting in violations; concealment of misconduct or falsification of required records; tampering with monitoring or control equipment; or business operation of pollution-related activities without a permit, license, manifest, or other required documentation. Corporate culpability may exist when a company performs an environmental compliance audit, identifies a violation, and then knowingly fails to remedy the noncompliance.

The DOJ US Attorneys' Manual includes a series of provisions governing the exercise of prosecutorial discretion with respect to business organizations. DOJ, U.S. Attorneys' Manual, § 9-28.000. Section 9-28.000 adopted the "Principles of Federal Prosecution of Business Organizations," which provide that corporations are not to be treated differently than individuals by virtue of their artificial nature, but that additional factors should be considered in determining whether to prosecute them. Factors to be considered must include:

1. The nature and seriousness of the offense, including the risk of harm to the public, and applicable policies and priorities, if any, governing the prosecution of corporations for particular categories of crime (*See* USAM 9-28.400)
2. The pervasiveness of wrongdoing within the corporation, including the complicity in, or the condoning of, the wrongdoing by corporate management (*See* USAM 9-28.500)
3. The corporation's history of similar misconduct, including prior criminal, civil, and regulatory enforcement actions against it (*See* USAM 9-28.600)
4. The corporation's timely and voluntary disclosure of wrongdoing and its willingness to cooperate in the investigation of its agents (*See* USAM 9-28.700)
5. The existence and effectiveness of the corporation's preexisting compliance program (*See* USAM 9-28.800)
6. The corporation's remedial actions, including any efforts to implement an effective corporate compliance program or to improve an existing one, to replace responsible management, to discipline or

terminate wrongdoers, to pay restitution, and to cooperate with the relevant government agencies (*See* USAM 9-28.900)

7. Collateral consequences, including whether there is disproportionate harm to shareholders, pension holders, employees, and others not proven personally culpable, as well as impact on the public arising from the prosecution (*See* USAM 9-28.1000)
8. The adequacy of the prosecution of individuals responsible for the corporation's malfeasance
9. The adequacy of remedies such as civil or regulatory enforcement actions (*See* USAM 9-28.1100)

These nine factors are critical to charging decisions and are often the subject of much debate between defense attorneys and prosecutors in environmental enforcement matters. One of the more controversial factors is consideration of the company's "willingness to cooperate." What constitutes cooperation has been the subject of significant controversy, federal legislation, and multiple revisions of DOJ policy. After highly contentious disputes with the defense bar, the DOJ clarified that waiver of the attorney-client privilege and work product protections were not prerequisites to finding that a company cooperated in the government's investigation. The US Attorneys' Manual now ostensibly prohibits prosecutors from requesting waiver as a condition of receiving cooperation credit.

Other publicly available resources can also factor into the exercise of investigative and prosecutorial discretion. EPA OCEFT's enforcement agreement guidance and the US Sentencing Commission's organizational sentencing guidelines are two good examples. Each provides a working model for what investigators and prosecutors expect from corporate environmental compliance programs.

EPA OCEFT's enforcement agreement guidance sets forth the key elements for a compliance-focused environmental management system (EMS) to be used in enforcement settlement agreements.[30] The guidance sets forth the twelve key elements of a "compliance-focused EMS":

[30] EPA OCEFT, EPA-330/9-97-002R, Compliance-Focused Environmental Management System – Enforcement Agreement Guidance (Rev. June 2005).

1. Environmental policy
2. Organization, personnel, and oversight of EMS
3. Accountability and responsibility
4. Environmental requirements
5. Assessment, prevention, and control
6. Environmental incident and noncompliance investigations
7. Environmental training, awareness, and competence
8. Environmental planning and organizational decision making
9. Maintenance of records and documentation
10. Pollution prevention
11. Continuing program evaluation and improvement
12. Public involvement/community outreach

The US Sentencing Commission's organizational sentencing guidelines are designed to provide incentives for organizations to detect and prevent crime. As pertinent, the guidelines define what constitutes an "effective compliance and ethics program," and organizations that meet the criteria can receive credit for reductions under the sentencing guidelines.[31] To have an "effective compliance and ethics program," an organization must (1) "exercise due diligence to prevent and detect criminal conduct" and (2) "otherwise promote an organizational culture that encourages ethical conduct and a commitment to compliance with the law." At a minimum, the program shall include:

1. Established standards and procedures to prevent and detect criminal conduct.
2. A governing authority that is knowledgeable about the content and operation of the compliance and ethics program and that exercises reasonable oversight with respect to the implementation and effectiveness of the compliance and ethics program.
3. High-level personnel that ensure that the organization has an effective compliance and ethics program with specific individual(s) assigned overall responsibility for the compliance and ethics program.
4. Specific individual(s) that have been delegated day-to-day operational responsibility for the compliance and ethics program;

[31] U.S. Sentencing Commission, Federal Sentencing Guidelines, § 8B2.1.

that report periodically to high-level personnel or to the governing authority on the effectiveness of the compliance and ethics program; and that have been provided adequate resources, appropriate authority, and direct access to the governing authority.

5. Reasonable efforts not to include within the substantial authority personnel of the organization any individual whom the organization knew, or should have known through the exercise of due diligence, has engaged in illegal activities or other conduct inconsistent with an effective compliance and ethics program.
6. Reasonable steps to communicate periodically and in a practical manner its standards and procedures, and other aspects of the compliance and ethics program, to the governing authority, high-level personnel, substantial authority personnel, the organization's employees, and as appropriate, the organization's agents, by conducting effective training programs and otherwise disseminating information appropriate to such individuals' respective roles and responsibilities.
7. Reasonable steps to ensure that the organization's compliance and ethics program is followed, including monitoring and auditing to detect criminal conduct; to evaluate periodically the effectiveness of the organization's compliance and ethics program; and to have and publicize a system, which may include mechanisms that allow for anonymity or confidentiality, whereby the organization's employees and agents may report or seek guidance regarding potential or actual criminal conduct without fear of retaliation.
8. Consistent promotion and enforcement of the compliance and ethics program throughout the organization through appropriate incentives to perform in accordance with the compliance and ethics program, and appropriate disciplinary measures for engaging in criminal conduct and for failing to take reasonable steps to prevent or detect criminal conduct.
9. Reasonable steps to detect and respond appropriately to any criminal conduct and to prevent further similar criminal conduct, including periodic assessment of the risk of criminal conduct; appropriate steps to design, implement, or modify each requirement of the compliance and ethics program; and necessary modifications to the organization's compliance and ethics program.

Although the organizational sentencing guidelines do not explicitly apply to corporate environmental cases, this definition nevertheless provides useful benchmarks and discussion points for both defense attorneys and prosecutors negotiating the resolution of corporate environmental enforcement matters.

There are any number of other publicly available resources that can also provide helpful insight.

An additional overlay worth mentioning is the fact that the EPA periodically selects "National Enforcement Initiatives" on which to focus its limited resources. These initiatives are revisited every three years to address some of what the EPA considers the more complex pollution problems through concentrated enforcement efforts. For fiscal years 2011 to 2013, the EPA identified six areas:

1. Keeping raw sewage and contaminated stormwater out of our nation's waters
2. Preventing animal waste from contaminating surface and ground waters
3. Cutting toxic air pollution that affects communities' health
4. Reducing widespread air pollution from the largest sources, especially the coal-fired utility, cement, glass, and acid sectors
5. Reducing pollution from mineral processing operations
6. Assuring energy extraction sector compliance with environmental laws[32]

The first five remain consistent with the initiatives selected for fiscal years 2008 to 2010. The addition of the sixth appears to be a function of the Obama administration's efforts to balance its clean energy goals. If climate change legislation or EPA greenhouse gas rules prompt a shift away from coal-fired power toward natural gas, then a resource extraction initiative could play a key role in mitigating potential groundwater contamination and air quality concerns. For example, the use of hydraulic fracturing as a means to stimulate natural gas production in shale has recently become a hot topic

[32] National Enforcement Initiatives for Fiscal Years 2011 - 2013, EPA.GOV, http://www.epa.gov/oecaerth/data/planning/initiatives/initiatives.html (last visited July 6, 2011).

in the administration given potential groundwater contamination concerns associated with certain fracturing practices.

DOJ ENRD periodically announces its own priorities as well. Assistant Attorney General Ignacia Moreno announced on January 13, 2011 that her department's "top enforcement priority is to hold fully accountable those responsible for the tragic loss and disastrous spill in the Gulf of Mexico."[33] Although DOJ ENRD filed a civil enforcement action in December 2010 against nine defendants alleged to have played roles in the spill, the DOJ later transferred jurisdiction over the criminal investigation from ENRD to the DOJ Criminal Division.[34] The rationale for, and impact of, the transfer remain unclear, but it may free up ENRD from having to allocate so many personnel to what will clearly be a resource-intensive investigation and potential prosecution.

Response Strategies and Parting Recommendations

Given the unique breadth of environmental law, enforcement authority is necessarily expansive, but not necessarily unbridled. Savvy practitioners in this area are familiar with the various guidance documents that govern the exercise of investigative and prosecutorial discretion, understand the scope of the current governmental enforcement initiatives, and appreciate what investigators and prosecutors should reasonably expect from corporate environmental compliance programs. Set forth below are four general recommendations for responding to an environmental enforcement action.

1. *Know Your Corporation.* Whether you are on the defense or on the prosecution, a thorough understanding of the corporation's inter-workings can be invaluable. Do not simply rely on representations of the state of compliance made by business managers or in-house counsel who may or may not have direct and routine communications with the field. Enforcement actions frequently arise out of miscommunications between those tasked with making

[33] Remarks as Prepared for Delivery by Assistant Attorney General Ignacia Moreno on 2011 Priorities for the Environment and Natural Resources Division (Jan. 13, 2011), (http://www.justice.gov/enrd/opa/pr/speeches/2011/enrd-speech-110113.html
[34] Carrie Johnson, *U.S. Overhauls Approach To BP Spill Probe*, NPR (March 24, 2011), http://www.npr.org/2011/03/24/134805501/u-s-overhauls-approach-to-bp-spill-probe

compliance representations on behalf of the company and those tasked with actual operations and environmental monitoring. Good defense attorneys partner directly with company engineers, operators, and environmental staff to field-verify material facts; to discern how the underlying technical processes can impact environmental compliance; and to develop a sense of the corporation's overall culture of compliance. These partnerships not only enhance the credibility of the defense attorney negotiating the matter with the government, but also help to identify and repair deficiencies in the compliance programs that may have led to the enforcement action. Good investigators and prosecutors seek working relationships with these defense attorneys, which can, in turn, allow the government to identify the root cause of the incident, giving rise to enforcement; to determine whether the matter is suitable for criminal or civil resolution; or to ascertain the extent to which injunctive relief is necessary.

2. *Find Common Ground.* More often than not, the government investigator and the defense attorney are similarly situated at the outset of enforcement matters, in that neither has a firm understanding of the actual events that led to the enforcement action. This is common ground. Increasingly, the government has become reliant on the results of corporate internal fact-finding investigations launched after the government's investigation. The companies seek credit for this cooperation; the government can reallocate its limited resources to more pressing enforcement initiatives; and judicial resources are preserved. Corporate internal investigative teams include environmental attorneys; air, water, and waste engineering consultants; and forensic e-discovery consultants to capture emissions data resident on complex data repositories like Supervisory Control and Data Acquisition (SCADA) systems. These teams work closely with the company in an attempt to resolve the government's concerns expeditiously and amicably.

3. *Recognize "Paper" Programs.* A common pitfall in the defense of environmental enforcement matters is undue reliance on a well-written, albeit poorly executed, EMS. Investigators and prosecutors are acutely aware of "Potemkin Village" environmental policies,

protocols, and programs. Meticulously constructed EMSs that have not been implemented are not accorded deference in investigative and prosecutorial decisions; can reflect more pervasive problems within the business organization; and often provide independent bases to expand the underlying investigation. An environmental policy statement drafted by a public relations firm is often just that—an environmental policy statement drafted by a public relations firm.

4. *Seek Just Results.* Zealous advocacy should be balanced with concerns for environmental impacts and the rights of the accused. Although this point should go without saying, it is worth reiterating. With respect to the former, curtailing environmental releases and mitigating any environmental harm must be the top priority. With respect to the latter, even corporations are entitled to a presumption of innocence. In criminal matters, prosecutors are and should be held to a higher standard of fairness, particularly given that life and liberty are in play. In 1935, in responding to a prosecutor that had overstepped the "bounds of propriety and justice," Justice George Sutherland penned the following in *U.S. v. Berger*:

> The United States Attorney is the representative not of an ordinary party to a controversy, but of a sovereignty whose obligation to govern impartially is as compelling as its obligation to govern at all, and whose interest, therefore, in a criminal case is not that it shall win a case, but that justice shall be done. As such, he is in a peculiar and very definite sense the servant of the law, the two-fold aim of which is that guilt shall not escape or innocence suffer. He may prosecute with earnestness and vigor – indeed he should do so. But while he may strike hard blows, he is not at liberty to strike foul ones.

295 U.S. 78, 85 (1935). This quote currently appears on a plaque posted in the DOJ ENRD. It was parting gift from Steve Solow, a former Chief of DOJ ENRD ECS.

On a final note, effective enforcement response will have benefits to both the corporation and the environment that run far beyond the given enforcement action. Experience has shown that closer management of environmental liabilities leads to lower costs on labor, energy, and material resources and to a lower environmental and financial risk profile. A more robust and defensible environmental compliance program may not only result in successful results to a specific enforcement initiative, but may also "green" the corporation's bottom line.

Key Takeaways

- Recognize that mitigating financial risks and environmental risks are not mutually exclusive: you can protect your shareholders and the air they breathe at the same time.
- Be wary of the fact that investigators and prosecutors have remarkable latitude in determining whether to initiate an investigation or to pursue a formal enforcement action.
- Familiarize yourself with the various guidance documents that govern the exercise of investigative and prosecutorial discretion.
- Understand the scope of current governmental enforcement initiatives and the extent to which they impact your client.
- Appreciate what investigators and prosecutors should reasonably expect from a corporate environmental compliance program in your client's industry.
- Consider the parting recommendations described above: (1) know your corporation, (2) find common ground, (3) recognize "paper" programs, and (4) seek just results.

Related Resources

- Memorandum from Earl E. Devaney, Director, EPA Office of Criminal Enforcement, to All Employees Working in or in Support of the Criminal Enforcement Program (Jan. 12, 1994) (regarding The Exercise of Investigative Discretion), *available at* http://www.epa.gov/compliance/resources/policies/criminal/exercise.pdf.

- DOJ, U.S. Attorneys' Manual, § 9-28.000, *available at* http://www.justice.gov/usao/eousa/foia_reading_room/usam/title9/28mcrm.htm.
- U.S. Sentencing Commission, Federal Sentencing Guidelines Manual, § 8B2.1, *available at* http://www.ussc.gov/Guidelines/010_guidelines/Manual_HTML/8b2_1.htm.
- EPA OCEFT, EPA-330/9-97-002R, Compliance-Focused Environmental Management System – Enforcement Agreement Guidance (Rev. June 2005), *available at* http://www.epa.gov/compliance/resources/policies/neic/cfems_05.pdf.

Karl R. Heisler is a partner in the Washington, D.C. office of Katten Muchin Rosenman LLP and a member of the firm's environmental team. His practice focuses on environmental and white collar law, with an emphasis on civil and criminal environmental enforcement. He regularly conducts internal investigations involving the Clean Water Act, the Clean Air Act, and the Resource Conservation and Recovery Act, among other environmental and worker safety regimes, and has experience defending clients facing obstruction of justice, false statements, and other Title 18 allegations.

Judicial Deference to Federal Administrative Agencies: Understanding the Landscape and Developing Strategies Accordingly

Sean M. Sullivan

Partner

Williams Mullen

ASPATORE

Introduction

Litigation is an expensive proposition, and the outcome of a trial is far from certain. As a result, business people would always prefer to negotiate a resolution. Now, imagine litigation where your threshold for victory is not the greater weight of the evidence but rather establishing that your opponent's position cannot be right. Such is the legal position in which most enforcement action targets find themselves. This chapter discusses why administrative agencies are in such an enviable legal position and the consequences of that position for: (1) handling an enforcement case already underway, and (2) relating to environmental regulators in a pre-enforcement context.

The EPA's Enforcement Process

Enforcement actions regarding environmental rules and regulations can arise in a variety of ways. In most states, state agencies are the organizations primarily responsible for ensuring compliance, and the Environmental Protection Agency (EPA) retains secondary authority to enforce most regulatory requirements. Even so, the EPA's status as the secondary enforcement authority does not prevent it from regularly initiating enforcement actions. In some jurisdictions, regional authorities and local governments will also have environmental rules, and the ability of state or federal regulators to enforce those requirements will depend on the particular program at issue.

The first step in an enforcement case is almost always an inspection. One or more agency personnel will arrive at a regulated facility, present their identification, and ask to speak to the individual responsible for environmental matters. In most cases, the inspection will be directed toward one particular set of rules, such as construction stormwater or the emission of air pollutants, but there is nothing to prevent a stormwater inspector from identifying violations of the hazardous waste rules other than his or her experience with those regulations. Facility personnel typically accompany inspectors during their visit, and there is normally a meeting at the conclusion of the inspection to discuss the inspector's findings. If the inspector identifies violations that are of more than a *de minimis* nature, the agency will usually follow up with a Notice of Violation (NOV). This is the first step in an enforcement case.

Once an enforcement action is underway, it typically proceeds in one of three ways. First, the environmental agency may attempt to negotiate a resolution of the case informally, without a formal administrative or judicial proceeding. Second, the agency may initiate a formal administrative action against a regulated party. Finally, the agency may file suit against the regulated party. In an informal negotiation, the agency will typically attempt to reach agreement on an administrative consent order that includes a monetary penalty as well as an order to comply with the regulations. If negotiations are unsuccessful, and depending upon the regulation at issue and the nature of the agency (federal, state, or local), the case will either evolve into a formal administrative action before an administrative law judge or it may proceed directly to court.

In most cases, the amount of the civil penalty to be assessed against the violator is the primary matter in dispute. A civil penalty has two components: the gravity-based component and the economic benefit component, and both components can be negotiated. The gravity-based portion of a penalty is intended to punish parties for a violation and to deter future violations, while the economic benefit portion is intended to deprive the regulated party of the economic benefit it realized from its failure to comply.

When negotiations fail, the primary driver for deciding between administrative or judicial enforcement is the agency's statutory authority to assess penalties and its ability to order a party to comply with the law. For example, the Clean Air Act and the Clean Water Act limit the value of any civil penalty the EPA can assess through an administrative proceeding. State laws can also have similar limitations on the ability of state and local agencies to assess civil penalties through an administrative proceeding.

The Basics of Judicial Deference to Federal Agencies

The concept of judicial deference to agencies arises from a simple maxim: judges are generalists who know the law, and agencies are the technical experts. Thus, with respect to rulemakings and administrative interpretations of the law, judicial review follows a two-step approach intended to recognize this distinction. As the Supreme Court explained in *Chevron, U.S.A. Inc. v. Natural Resources Defense Council*:

> First, always, is the question whether Congress has directly spoken to the precise question at issue. If the intent of Congress is clear, that is the end of the matter; for the court, as well as the agency, must give effect to the unambiguously expressed intent of Congress. If, however, the court determines Congress has not directly addressed the precise question at issue, the court does not simply impose its own construction on the statute, as would be necessary in the absence of an administrative interpretation. Rather, if the statute is silent or ambiguous with respect to the specific issue, the question for the court is whether the agency's answer is based on a permissible construction of the statute.

467 U.S. 837, 842-43 (1984). Regarding an agency's factual determinations, a reviewing court must accept them so long as they are supported by "substantial evidence." 5 U.S.C. § 706(2)(E). In other words, so long as an agency does not run afoul of the plain meaning of a statute, and so long as there is enough evidence to make out a rational case for an agency's factual conclusions, a court will not disturb them (the Doctrine of Deference).

EPA Enforcement Procedures and the Applicability of the Doctrine of Deference

As noted above, if a regulated party does not reach an informal administrative settlement of an enforcement case, the next step is either a formal administrative action or a judicial enforcement action. Unfortunately, the Doctrine of Deference applies differently in each scenario.

In a formal administrative action involving the EPA, an administrative law judge (ALJ) will hear evidence and legal arguments, make findings of fact and conclusions of law at the end of the proceeding, and issue an "Initial Order." *See* 40 C.F.R. § 22.27. If dissatisfied with the outcome of the hearing, a regulated party has thirty days to seek review of the Initial Order before the

Environmental Appeals Board (EAB).[1] *See* 40 C.F.R. § 22.30(a). The EAB may also decide to review an Initial Order within forty-five days of the date of the Initial Order. *See* 40 C.F.R. § 22.30(b) At the conclusion of the appeal to the EAB, the Board will issue a Final Order. A regulated party can then seek judicial review of the Final Order in federal district court.

Judicial review of a Final Order from the EAB requires a court to evaluate the factual conclusions reflected in the Final Order as well as the EAB's conclusions of law. In this scenario, a reviewing court applies the substantial evidence test to the agency's factual conclusions and it reviews the conclusions of law in accordance with *Chevron*. As a result, private parties face a significant uphill battle when attempting to overturn the result of a formal administrative enforcement case in federal court.

In cases where the EPA proceeds directly to a judicial enforcement action, the landscape is different. The *court* will make the relevant findings of fact and conclusions of law, not the EPA. To the extent that the EPA has published guidance or other interpretations of its regulations, those interpretations may be entitled to some deference, but the court will not be conducting a *Chevron* review of the EPA's decision. Instead, it will be applying the law to the facts of the case for the first time.

Implications for Defending an Enforcement Case Brought by the EPA

I divide enforcement cases and allegations of noncompliance into three basic types: (1) ones in which the violation occurred and the issue is the amount of the penalty; (2) ones in which there is a factual dispute over whether a violation occurred; and (3) ones in which a disputed interpretation of a legal requirement will determine if a violation occurred. In addition, it is critical to know the potential financial exposure that accompanies an enforcement action, the likely venue for a formal enforcement case (administrative versus judicial), and a rough estimate of the cost to litigate the case in an administrative or judicial forum (or both). With this information, the appropriate strategy for proceeding becomes clear. For example, litigating the merits of a case in which the EPA's

[1] If a regulated party fails to appeal an ALJ's Initial Order to the EAB, the party is prohibited from seeking judicial review of the case in federal court. *See* 40 C.F.R. § 22.27(d).

proposed civil penalty is $50,000 and the costs of coming into compliance are minimal would not make much sense. But, in the context of a New Source Review enforcement case, the costs to retrofit pollution controls can easily exceed $10 million, and a regulated entity may have more of an incentive to litigate, depending on the facts.

Cases Where Only the Penalty Amount is in Dispute

For most of the EPA's regulatory programs, the agency's Office of Enforcement and Compliance Assurance (OECA) has developed a penalty policy that describes the way in which the EPA calculates penalties for violations of its rules. Copies of the policies are available on OECA's website. For the gravity-based portion of a penalty, the EPA typically uses a matrix based on the extent to which the violator deviated from the requirement and the potential harm that could arise from the alleged violation. The EPA can then adjust the penalty upward or downward based on fact-specific issues such as: (1) a quick return to compliance; (2) cooperation with the investigation; (3) good faith efforts to comply or knowing/intentional violations; and (4) quick settlement. For the economic benefit portion of a penalty, the EPA may have predetermined the amount for each violation—based on a general financial analysis by OECA—or the agency may do a case-specific analysis. Regulated parties are free to provide their own evidence of economic benefit (or lack thereof) from the alleged violation.

In this scenario, an informally negotiated consent agreement is likely the preferred outcome, and the EPA's discretion is at its greatest. Aside from persuading the agency regarding the factors described above, other effective strategies include analogizing to sample penalty calculations in the penalty policy that produce more favorable results and arguing that the agency's calculation unfairly penalizes a regulated party. For example, in a situation where one act or omission triggers a number of violations and the EPA proposes to assess a penalty for each such violation, pointing to a party's good faith efforts to comply is an effective strategy for persuading the agency to back away from these so-called "cascading violations."

In cases where there is no disagreement as to the existence of a violation, administrative or judicial litigation is not advisable unless the EPA's calculation of the penalty amount is grossly out of line with the penalty policy. ALJs and district court judges typically follow the EPA's penalty policies, and if a case proceeds to litigation, the opportunity to receive a penalty reduction for cooperation or quick settlement is usually gone.

Cases Where There is a Factual Dispute Regarding an Alleged Violation

EPA inspectors are human and they make mistakes. Moreover, from the EPA's perspective, alleged violations with questionable evidentiary support are good giveaways in a negotiation. As a result, it is better to address these types of allegations before beginning substantive negotiations on a penalty amount. By doing so, regulated parties can limit the effect of these allegations on their overall negotiating leverage and they can make a strong showing to the agency's enforcement personnel as to their willingness to defend the case.

If informal discussions with the EPA are unsuccessful in resolving factual disputes, regulated parties must evaluate the costs of administrative or judicial litigation and determine whether it makes sense to settle or not. Either way, persuading the person who will make the original findings of fact is the key. A federal court will not overturn the EPA's findings of fact in an administrative proceeding unless the court can say there is not enough evidence for the EPA to have rationally reached its conclusion. Nor will an appellate court overturn a district court's findings of fact.

Cases Where There is a Legal Dispute Regarding an Alleged Violation

The EPA's website is filled with guidance explaining the requirements of its regulations, most of which has never been subject to notice and comment procedures created by the Administrative Procedure Act. Nonetheless, the agency commonly treats this guidance as binding on the regulated community, even though the EPA has adopted contradictory interpretations of a number of its rules at different times over the past thirty years. The keys to resolving an interpretative dispute of this type are: (1) gauging whether a reviewing court would defer to the interpretation advanced by the agency, and (2) appreciating the effect of a loss by the EPA on the agency's regulatory program. The greater the risk of loss, and the greater the effect that a loss would have on a particular program, the less likely the EPA is to press an interpretative point.

Implications of the Doctrine of Deference When Seeking Guidance from the EPA and State Environmental Agencies

To be sure, the Doctrine of Deference affords the EPA great flexibility in an enforcement context. It also affords the agency significant flexibility in applying regulations to a particular situation when the regulated community seeks guidance. For example, 40 C.F.R. § 261.6(c)(2) allows facilities to recycle hazardous waste without obtaining a Treatment, Storage, and Disposal facility permit so long as the facility does not "store" hazardous wastes prior to recycling them. But when is a recycling facility "storing" hazardous waste? In the notice of proposed rulemaking for Section 261.6, the EPA suggested a holding period of up to two to three weeks might be permissible. In guidance, the EPA has stated that hazardous wastes can only be held for twenty-four hours before recycling begins, but the agency has also approved state regulatory programs that allow storage for up to forty-eight hours. Plus, does storage prior to recycling begin when a delivery truck arrives at a recycling facility or only when the hazardous wastes are removed from the truck and brought into the facility itself?

To the extent that regulations do not compel a specific result, ambiguity affords the regulated community an opportunity to persuade an agency to interpret rules in a favorable way. Continuing with the example above, a private party may be able to persuade an agency to allow a facility to "hold" hazardous waste for several days but not considering that "holding" to be "storage," depending on the nature of the facility and the waste involved. So long as the ultimate interpretation is not plainly contradictory to the applicable regulations, it is unlikely that a court would reject it.

Conclusion

In an enforcement context, regulated parties are fighting an uphill battle against the EPA. By recognizing this fact early on and interacting with the agency accordingly, you stand a better chance of being able to: (1) negotiate an acceptable resolution of alleged violations, and (2) keep the EPA's mind open regarding factual disputes and interpretative issues. If negotiations are approaching an impasse, a clear understanding of your burdens of proof—and the presumptions in favor of the EPA—will allow you to make a more informed decision about whether to walk away from the negotiating table.

Key Takeaways

- In an environmental enforcement case, EPA has the benefit of knowing that a court will defer to the agency in most situations. The earlier you can convince EPA about a factual or legal issue, the better, and maintaining a good working relationship with EPA's personnel will assist you in doing so.
- Understanding the nature of the dispute with EPA, the potential financial exposure that accompanies an environmental enforcement action, the likely venue for a formal enforcement case—i.e., administrative versus judicial—and a rough estimate of the cost to litigate the case is critical. Based on this information, the appropriate strategy for proceeding becomes clear.
- Providing your own evidence of the economic benefits from an alleged violation can be an effective strategy of mitigating that portion of a civil penalty. Analogizing to sample penalty calculations that produce more favorable results and arguing that the agency's calculation unfairly penalizes a regulated party are effective strategies for negotiating gravity-based penalties.
- Addressing alleged violations with questionable evidentiary support before beginning substantive negotiations with the EPA on a penalty amount is a good idea, as it can help to limit the effect of these allegations on your client's overall negotiating leverage and demonstrates your willingness to defend the case.
- While the Doctrine of Deference can make defending enforcement cases more difficult, it also provides an opportunity when seeking guidance from EPA in non-adversarial situations.

Related Resources:

EPA Guidance

U.S. EPA, Office of Administrative Law Judges, Practice Manual (May 2009), *available at* http://www.epa.gov/aljhomep/orders/alj-practice-manual.pdf.

U.S. EPA, Environmental Appeals Board, Practice Manual (Sept. 2010), *available at* http://yosemite.epa.gov/oa/EAB_Web_Docket.nsf/ 8f612ee7 fc725edd852570760071cb8e/0d39a701f36642af8525788000414195/$FILE/PracticeManual%202010.pdf.

Consolidated Rules of Practice Governing Administrative Assessment of Civil Penalties and the Revocation/Termination or Suspension of Permits, 40 C.F.R. Part 22, *available at* http://www.epa.gov/aljhomep/rules/crop.pdf.

U.S. EPA, Civil Penalty Policies, *available at* http://cfpub.epa.gov/compliance/resources/policies/civil/penalty/ (last visited June 13, 2011).

Judicial Decisions of Note

Chevron U.S.A. Inc. v. Natural Resources Defense Council, 467 U.S. 837 (1984) (discussing *Chevron* deference).

United States v. Mead Corp., 533 U.S. 218 (2001) (describing rules for deference to agency guidance and determinations not subject to notice and comment procedures).

Enforcement Provisions of Major Environmental Statutes

Clean Air Act – 42 U.S.C. § 7413

Clean Water Act – 33 U.S.C. § 1319

Comprehensive Environmental Response Compensation and Liability Act – 42 U.S.C. §§ 9606 & 9609

Emergency Planning and Community Right to Know Act – 42 U.S.C. § 11045
Federal Insecticide Fungicide and Rodenticide Act – 7 U.S.C. §§ 136K & 136L

Resource Conservation and Recovery Act (Hazardous Waste) – 42 U.S.C. § 6928

Resource Conservation and Recovery Act (Underground Storage Tanks) – 42 U.S.C. § 6991e

Toxic Substances Control Act – 15 U.S.C. § 2615

Sean M. Sullivan is a partner in Williams Mullen's environmental section. His practice involves auditing, compliance counseling, and enforcement defense regarding all of the major federal environmental statutes, due diligence and permit transfers for corporate transactions, and judicial review of federal agency actions and rulemakings. Mr. Sullivan also represents clients involved in toxic tort litigation as well as CERCLA information requests, response actions, and cost recovery actions.

Mr. Sullivan is licensed to practice in the District of Columbia, Florida, North Carolina, and Virginia and before the US Supreme Court. He is a member of the Section on Natural Resources and Environment of the American Bar Association and serves as vice-chair of the ABA's Committee on Pesticides, Chemical Regulation, and Right to Know. In addition, Mr. Sullivan is active in the Section Council of the Natural Resources and Environment Section of the North Carolina Bar Association and serves as course planner for the 2011 Section Annual Meeting. He is a member of the Carolinas Air Pollution Control Association and Coastal Carolina Tomorrow, an organization dedicated to the preservation of life that exists in southeastern North Carolina's coastal communities, as well as the National Retail Federation's Committee on Sustainability and Environmental Compliance.

Mr. Sullivan received his juris doctor, cum laude, from American University's Washington College of Law in 2001. While in law school, Mr. Sullivan served as recent developments editor of the Administrative Law Review *and assistant director of the Moot Court Board. He was a dean's fellow of the National Equal Justice Library and a judicial intern to the Honorable Joan Zeldon of the D.C. Superior Court. Mr. Sullivan received his Bachelor of Science degree in environmental science, with honors, from the University of Miami in 1998.*

Workforce Training and Other Key Aspects of Environmental Law Compliance

Nicolle R. Snyder Bagnell

Partner

Reed Smith LLP

ASPATORE

Introduction

The purpose of this chapter is to provide practical advice and pointers to counsel, both within corporations and outside of them, who are interested in positioning their clients well in advance of, and hopefully to entirely avoid, an environmental enforcement action. From my experience, one of the most important ways to have a good plan in place that avoids or mitigates violations is for the attorneys to understand their clients' businesses, be familiar with the processes and where potential violations may arise, and to work together with the people actually doing the processes, be it manufacturing, oil and gas development, or anything else that is regulated by environmental law.

Recent Changes in Environmental Law Enforcement Practices

The amount of attention paid to environmental law and regulations has been evolving over the ten years that I have been practicing in this field, and certainly well before I entered the practice. Companies are increasingly trying to ensure that their corporate plans and policies are in compliance with all aspects of environmental law for both environmental and business reasons. As a result, there is a very important role for those involved in the practice of environmental law to ensure that compliance training and response plans are in place to avoid any violation of environmental law or to address a potential violation quickly in the event of an accident or mistake in this area.

Essentially, while in the past it might have been true that enforcement agencies targeted individuals or companies who were continuously out of compliance with the law, that does not happen very often today because most corporations seek to comply with the law and be good environmental citizens. Therefore, it is important for everyone in a company—and not just the people at the top of a corporation—to understand the specific environmental laws that affect their business. Most importantly, a company must strive to avoid the impacts to the environment, the public, and to the company itself of noncompliance in the event that something does go wrong. Even though most clients are already complying or attempting to comply with the law, enforcement training still plays a very important role. Consequently, an environmental law enforcement strategy is a tool that is useful in terms of aiding compliance at every level of a company.

Key Agencies Participating in Environmental Law Enforcement Cases

The government agencies that participate in environmental law enforcement cases are generally specific to a particular industry area. For example, in the oil and natural gas industry in Pennsylvania, where I practice, environmental lawyers typically deal with enforcement at every level of both state and federal enforcement. Not only do we deal with the state Department of Environmental Protection (DEP), we also work with other government agencies in Pennsylvania that have been involved in a significant amount of regulation and enforcement. A number of river basins, which can be part of inner state or inter county coalitions, are getting involved in the regulatory aspects of environmental law. Other state agencies such as the Pennsylvania Fish and Boat Commission have been enforcing the laws pertaining to water pollution in new ways. These agencies have always had a focus on water pollution that affected fish and fisheries, but that role is now expanding beyond simply protecting fish to regulating all unpermitted discharges. Essentially, all levels of government agencies are increasingly involved in environmental law enforcement.

In addition, the Environmental Protection Agency (EPA) is often involved in state actions pertaining to air and water pollution. Even in those cases where a state agency is taking the lead in a compliance action, the EPA has also been highly focused on determining what was happening in terms of gathering information, and deciding if they were going to initiate an independent enforcement action. It should be noted that public attention can play a role in potential enforcement actions. For example, there has undoubtedly been increased attention given to the oil and gas industry throughout the United States as a result of the oil spill in the Gulf of Mexico and the problems faced by the nuclear energy industry in Japan. A great deal of media and political attention has been focused on energy industries, and the EPA has taken the lead in many of these investigations. On the state level, politicians and the public are talking about environmental law enforcement and state regulators are increasing their enforcement efforts.

Helping Clients Understand the Importance of Compliance

I believe that the goal of most companies is to comply with the law in this area, as doing so is in their best interest on many levels. Being in compliance with environmental laws is important in terms of a responsible corporate citizen. Being in compliance with environmental law helps companies get their work done quickly, efficiently, and safely; therefore, there is an economic component to compliance, as well as considerations for worker health and safety. Finally, compliance with environmental law is critical to the public's perception and support for the company.

Of course, mistakes are always going to be made in any industry—and one concept that many clients fail to understand is the fact that environmental compliance is not just a matter of paying a penalty when you commit a violation. In fact, there is a very real possibility that your business—whatever industry you are in—will be shut down because of a violation of environmental law. In most cases, it will be a temporary shutdown while an investigation is taking place, but in the past year I have seen a number of instances where a state agency has taken an aggressive line in enforcement and has shut down a company's entire operations within the state where it is located. Consequently, I think that it is very important for clients to understand that they should not only be concerned about how much money a violation is going to cost them; more importantly, they might be subject to a shutdown.

I believe that the best way to help a client to understand the importance of environmental law compliance is by giving them examples of enforcement actions that have occurred in their jurisdiction or region. For instance, I might explain to a client what happened in a recent case, or analyze how a government agency is approaching a pending case, because doing so helps the client get a sense of what is happening to other people in their own industry or in their region, and it also helps them understand the approaches that the current administrations of the agencies that regulate their industry are taking. Simply stated, ensuring compliance in this area is not only a matter of knowing what the regulations are, it is a matter of knowing how those regulations are going to be enforced by a particular state agency during the time period when you are doing business.

Unique Aspects of the Environmental Law Enforcement Process

On the lowest level of environmental law enforcement there are reporting requirements unique to the industry that provide the regulating body with information that they can review to determine whether or not an entity is acting in compliance with its permits, rules, and regulations. In most instances, mandatory reporting is coupled with periodic (and often unannounced) inspections undertaken on the state and federal levels. Both of those activities allow the relevant regulatory agency to have an idea of what is going on within corporations, how they function, what their processes are, what laws govern them, and what the potential sources of violations may be. If there is evidence of a violation or a potential violation, there will typically be a ramped-up, full-fledged investigation concerning what was going on within the company. At that point, state and federal agencies have the ability to come into a company and inspect the facility as well as interview people, or they can ask for written responses to specific questions. Next, they may issue a penalty or require the client to take some additional action. Following the enactment of a penalty and an evaluation of that penalty, there may be settlement discussions, and ultimately, there might be a trial or a hearing on the viability or validity of the penalties that were issued.

When a violation is discovered, one key item both the enforcers in this area and the entity against which the violation is alleged need to examine is whether a particular violation arises from an accident or incident that is essentially a onetime thing—i.e., a violation arising from the fact that a rogue employee was doing something they were not supposed to do—or whether the violation is the result of a systemic problem within the company. If the cause is the latter, the company may need to implement wholesale changes to their environmental procedures or policies, and increase training for their employees. Therefore, a primary distinction in this area of enforcement from others is trying to decide what is the ultimate source of the alleged violation.

The Information Gathering Process

I believe that the most important thing a lawyer can do when they are trying to help a client comply with environmental laws and regulations is to learn everything that they can about the client's business, because it is very important to be able to spot potential issues—and you can only do that by knowing what is really going on in the client's company. Obviously, a lawyer may not be able to understand all of the intricacies of every industry that their clients work in, but they should obtain a general understanding of the manufacturing or other processes that their client utilizes and how they work.

Ultimately, in addition to identifying for yourself what you believe a client's environmental issues may be, it is a good idea to ask the client what they think their current compliance issues are. In most cases, I have found that it is not enough to simply talk to a client; rather, one of the most useful things that a lawyer can do is to actually go out and look at a manufacturing or production process in operation and see how it works in order to fully understand what is going on at the client's company. It is one thing to read about a manufacturing or production process on paper, but it is another thing entirely to go out to the field and see how it works in practice. Not only do you get a better idea of the manufacturing or production process and what causes certain types of environmental waste, but you also get to observe the people in the workforce who are undertaking those activities, and doing so gives you a much better idea of how to come up with a plan to avoid violations.

In fact, I believe that the biggest factors involved in avoiding environmental violations is to have a well-trained workforce who understands the environmental regulations that apply to their industry and why they need to comply with them, and to then implement a practical approach to compliance. It is not good enough to simply say to your workforce, "Don't allow this emission to occur." Rather, there must be a process for avoiding emissions that is built into the way the company's compliance system is set up. At the same time, if the people at the plant cannot successfully implement that compliance process, then no one has done their work effectively. Consequently, environmental lawyers need to work with the company to determine what changes need to be made to the company's compliance process, equipment, or production design. Certainly, lawyers cannot make those changes on their own, but they can help to bring these issues to the attention of the company and get them addressed.

Client Compliance Concerns

I have found that clients are typically most concerned with understanding what the law is in this area, and how it applies to them so that they can comply with it. Again, I believe that the goal for most clients is not to know the law in order to avoid complying with it; in most cases, they want to know the law so that they can do what needs to be done. Therefore, our clients' biggest concern involves both understanding the law in this area and knowing that all of their employees have a level of understanding that makes compliance possible.

In addition, compliance with environmental law is not simply a matter of having the type of equipment that complies with the law—it requires active oversight of processes that are regulated and work to make sure that things are functioning property. Unfortunately, there are scenarios where the law is not necessarily written in such a way as to make compliance possible. For example, there are times when a company's process is functioning perfectly and it is still exceeding a set air emission limit. Consequently, I believe that there needs to be a greater understanding on the part of both clients and regulators regarding what certain industries typically do and what their production/manufacturing processes entail so that environmental regulations can be written in such a way that they are able to be met, and they are practical in terms of the processes they apply to.

Fortunately, I think that regulators generally make efforts to enact compliance requirements that are practical and can be met and lawmaking provides an opportunity for the public, including the industry to be regulated, to provide comments on proposed laws and regulations. At the same time, as new processes are implemented on a statewide level that need to be regulated, it is important for regulators to meet with industry leaders so that everyone knows how those new processes work and how they can be regulated effectively. Industries tend to be best regulated when industry regulators fully understand the processes that are used in those industries, they are focusing on those areas that really need to be regulated, and they then regulate them in a way that is effective and efficient.

Compliance Training for the Client's Workforce

Compliance training for the client's workforce is perhaps the most important aspect of preventing environmental law violations, as previously noted. Essentially, there needs to be a regular and useful training program at the client company that correctly trains people in the jobs that they actually do, and that makes the training process specific to those individuals. For example, it is not enough to train a new employee generally on environmental law or on all the processes that a company is involved in—the training must be specific to that employee's job.

At the same time, it is important to make sure that the training process is frequently updated. Many companies conduct a training program for employees when they first start working at the company. However, I liken this type of training to when I was first trained on using my work computer; it was not until I was actually trying to write and save my first document that I thought of the right questions to ask—and that was well after the training process was over. Therefore, while it is a good idea to have some initial safety or environmental training when an employee first starts working, that training needs to be continuous so that the client's workforce has an opportunity to ask questions and learn more about their jobs once they know more about what is involved in the work process.

Working with Company Leaders

In order to develop an effective environmental law compliance strategy you must learn all that you can about the client's business and its processes, as previously noted, and then, with the help of the client, you need to identify potentially applicable environmental regulations. It is always extremely helpful to locate effective point people within the client's company who can help their lawyers to understand what their operational process consists of, and what happens if, in fact, a violation occurs. Those same company leaders should be able to help the workers who are doing the day-to-day tasks within the company when they have questions and issues they want to raise.

Typically, the components of a compliance strategy or document do not need to be updated too frequently, unless there is a change in government regulations or in company processes. However, if the person who was previously the point person with respect to environmental law compliance moves on, is promoted, or goes to a different job, it is important to identify who the next point person will be so that there is no gap in terms of knowing who can answer those key compliance questions, or who will be involved in environmental decision making at any point.

Consequently, in order to help a client develop an effective compliance strategy, you need to learn their business and be in contact with the key personnel who can help identify what the client's compliance issues are. The client needs to be the driver in putting together a compliance plan. Developing the plan is the lawyer's job, but the client needs to tell you what the plan has to include, because they best know their business.

Initial Steps after Receiving a Notice of Violation

The first step to take after a client receives a notice of violation (NOV) is information gathering. You have to figure out what happened, why it happened, when it happened, and whether it is actually a violation. In fact, just because some incident occurred and things did not work out as they should have, that does not necessarily mean that there was a violation. Indeed, in some cases, before a NOV is sent out, the regulating agency may ask for information about the incident in order to determine if a violation actually occurred.

Generally, after the client receives a notice of violation there is an opportunity for the client to respond, either in writing or in person, to the allegations in the notice. Therefore, after assembling all of the facts pertaining to the case, you will need to develop a response strategy. In some cases, you may want to approach the agency about a possible resolution, or if you are sure that the client did not commit a violation, you may want to immediately file an appeal as soon as that is practical. If your strategy involves settlement discussions, you need to contact the applicable regulatory agency, but it up to them to set a timeline for the case. Likewise, if you decide to fight the NOV, you will need to go through a court or hearing board process, depending on the nature of the alleged violation.

Unfortunately, I find that both clients and lawyers tend to immediately react to a NOV by deciding what the appropriate legal response should be in terms of how to fight it. However, I believe that doing your homework and knowing the facts are the most important steps in these cases and must always be done first, because knowing and understanding the facts can change the client's mind about how they want to respond—and it can also change the regulator's mind regarding how they want to proceed with respect to an alleged violation. For instance, if you learn that the violation was caused by a piece of equipment breaking down and it was a onetime event, and you then share that information with the agency, they are likely to pursue enforcement in a very different way than if your investigation shows that the client committed this type of violation on a regular basis.

Dealing with Enforcement Agencies

Developing a strategy for dealing with environmental law enforcement agencies is highly dependent on the particular case you are dealing with. For instance, if a person within the state agency who deals with air pollution issues has sent your client an air pollution violation notice, it may be best for your internal expert to work directly with the regulating agency's expert in order to try to understand the client's production process and what potentially went wrong with it. It should be noted that I have observed few differences between working with a federal agency as opposed to a state or local environmental law enforcement agency. The process is usually the same (i.e., there is a request for information and in-person meetings).

With respect to negotiating the terms of a settlement, the lawyer needs to be directly involved with the regulatory agency. Alternatively, if the key issue is how the client's operating process can be changed, it is important to get the person involved on the corporate side together with the person at the regulatory agency so that they can talk about the issue. Of course, once you are dealing with an alleged violation, lawyers are going to be involved in the process as well, but unlike the case in other types of law enforcement, there is generally a need for the people on the ground—i.e., the individuals who are doing the work in terms of regulatory and compliance actions—to talk to each other.

Developing Creative Responses to Environmental Law Compliance Challenges

Perhaps one of the greatest challenges of this practice area is the complexity of the law. It is often difficult to understand how the regulations in this area apply to a client's business. This can be particularly challenging for smaller businesses that do not typically have entire teams of people who are working on environmental compliance. Consequently, I often have to engage in a lot of explanatory discussions with clients regarding how the law works, particularly for industries that are frequently subject to new regulations, or new enforcement of old regulations.

In order to best position their companies to meet compliance requirements, I believe that clients really need to focus on training their workforce, as previously noted. In the past, companies might have had an environmental compliance officer or head of environmental compliance as their only point of environmental compliance. That compliance strategy is no longer sufficient for most industries, however. Rather, I think that everyone who works in the company needs to have an understanding of what environmental law compliance entails. They do not need to know every detail, but they should have an understanding of what the environmental requirements are that pertain to their company, why they are important, and what needs to be done in order to comply with them. Again, if the head of environmental compliance knows that you are not supposed to be doing something, but the worker who is in charge of implementing a particular compliance process does not understand why it is important, then there has been a real breakdown in communication—and a real potential for noncompliance.

Correctly implementing compliance measures can be costly, because a company needs to pay for compliance training, and there is lost work time while the workforce is being educated. However, compliance training programs pay off for companies in the long run, because they can help to avoid compliance issues.

Advising Clients on Costs and Timeline Issues

It is difficult to advise a client up front regarding the costs involved with environmental law compliance issues, because those issues are going to be different for every group you work with. To make a well-founded estimate, you need to know details about the company and its processes. Ultimately, however, the results of an environmental law noncompliance violation can be much greater than simply paying a penalty; they can have lasting impacts on your business from a public perception standpoint. Being cast as a violator may affect getting certain permits in the future, and as noted, it can even result in a shutdown. Conversely, the costs of implementing a compliance strategy and training program are usually much lower that the costs resulting from a notice of violation.

The timeframe involved between the time a client receives a notice of violation and the time the violation is resolved can take many years. Even in cases where a company agrees that they will pay a penalty and strive to do better in the future, a case may take three to four months to resolve. Alternatively, if the client does not believe that they committed a violation, the time it takes to fight an alleged violation can be lengthy.

Legal Issues Facing Clients Operating in Multiple Locations

Clients who have facilities throughout the nation or the world face many additional challenges when it comes to compliance with environmental laws and regulations. Consequently, it is not enough, as previously noted, to have one environmental compliance person who works at company headquarters; you need to have such an individual in most, if not all, of the company's facilities. In most cases, even if some environmental laws are the same in different states or regions, the enforcement of those laws may be different, and the compliance measures in relation to those laws will be different as well—and that can even be true with respect to facilities within the same state, but in different areas of that state.

Therefore, you really need to know and understand what the regulators who are on the ground expect and how they want you to comply with the law, and the only way to achieve that goal is to have someone at each corporate location who serves as a critical point person—someone who knows how the business works and how it is being regulated, and who can be the face of the company for the regulators in that area. The same rule applies to multinational companies; I cannot imagine how difficult it would be to know and understand the intricacies and complexities of environmental compliance for business operations in more than one country—it is hard enough to understand the rules in more than one state.

Anticipated Changes and New Strategies in Environmental Law Enforcement

Looking ahead, I believe that there is going to be increased environmental law enforcement, particularly in the area where I practice—largely because there has been so much media coverage and political interest in natural gas production, which despite a long history of development in Pennsylvania has recently enjoyed a resurgence. Oil and gas operations have been going on in Pennsylvania for more than one hundred years, and it was also the first state to have natural gas production facilities, but the regulations in this area are still developing—and as they continue to develop, enforcement is likely to increase.

In order to keep our clients informed of changes in this area, our firm has an environmental blog that we use to send our clients frequent updates on changes in the law. For those clients who I work with on a regular basis, whenever there has been a significant change in the law I generally keep them informed through an e-mail or a personal call. We also conduct training programs and luncheons for clients and non-clients to help business people who are being regulated understand the regulations that apply to their company.

I believe that the best piece of advice that I can give to other lawyers in this practice area is, again, to learn all that you can about the industries that you are representing. Young lawyers tend to think that all they need to know about is the law in their area—which is correct, but it is not enough. They also need to know about how their client companies work, because you cannot apply the law and create an effective legal strategy if you do not understand the company you are representing. You need to understand the client's business and their motivations, including why and how they do things, because if you do not, you might think that you have achieved a great outcome for them—when in fact you may have negotiated a settlement with which the client cannot comply. It may turn out that the client did not have to pay a particular penalty, or they have promised to do something going forward that they cannot fulfill. I think it is important for lawyers to avoid the tendency to just sit in their offices, and instead go out in the field and learn about the industries they are working for.

Conclusion

Ultimately, I believe that enforcement plays a very important role in the environmental arena, and when done properly, the result is typically reasonable and often helps an industry to grow in an environmentally sound manner. At the same time, it is important for regulators and industry leaders to work together to do the work that needs to be done in an efficient and environmentally sound way.

Key Takeaways

- Working with a client to help them comply with environmental law and regulations entails learning everything that you can about the client's business. In order to spot potential issues you need to know what is really going on in the client's company, including the manufacturing or other processes the client utilizes and how they work.
- Preventing environmental law violations is more likely if you help your client company create a training program that correctly trains people in their jobs, and which makes the training process specific to those individuals. It is also important to make sure that the training process is frequently updated.
- Locate effective point people within the client company who can help you to understand what their operational process consists of, and what happens if, in fact, a violation occurs. Those same company leaders should be able to help the workers who are doing the day-to-day tasks within the company when they have questions and issues they want to raise.
- Gathering information is important after a client receives a notice of an alleged violation. You have to figure out what happened, why it happened, when it happened, and whether it is actually a violation.
- Effective compliance strategies are most easily achieved when companies and their counsel work together to create practical and effective programs and procedures for companies to follow.

Nicolle R. Snyder Bagnell is a partner at Reed Smith LLP in Pittsburgh. Ms. Bagnell has an AB from Harvard University, an MA from the Nicholas School of the Environment at Duke University, and a JD from Duke University School of Law. She has been selected as a "Pennsylvania Rising Star" by Pennsylvania Super Lawyers from 2005 to 2010. Ms. Bagnell was also recognized as one of Law 360's 10 Energy Attorneys Under 40 to Watch.

Ms. Bagnell is a member of Reed Smith's Environmental team within the Global Regulatory Enforcement Group. Her experience includes counseling clients on a variety of environmental matters, such as performing due diligence for large real estate transactions, advising clients on compliance with environmental regulations, and representing energy clients in various matters, particularly pipeline condemnations, encroachment cases, and various contract disputes. She is actively involved in litigation and regulatory issues regarding the Marcellus Shale in Appalachia, counseling clients on permitting and permit disputes, representing industry groups and producers in Minimum Royalty Act litigation and many other lease disputes, and performing due diligence and providing advice for Marcellus Shale transactions. Ms. Bagnell has been named the Oil and Gas Chair for the Energy and Mineral Law Foundation's 32nd Annual Institute.

Knowing the Law and Knowing Your Client: Keys to Success in the Practice of Environmental Law

Carol Clayton and Kenneth Meade

Partners

Wilmer Cutler Pickering Hale and Dorr LLP

ASPATORE

Introduction

Environmental law is a thicket of dense, overlapping, and sometimes inconsistent federal and state statutes, regulations, case law, and agency guidance documents. Penalties for non-compliance can be severe, including substantial civil and criminal fines, and imprisonment for responsible corporate officers and other individuals who commit an environmental crime. Perhaps the most unique aspects of this practice area are the multiple enforcement agencies that can be and often are involved in a client's case, the multiplicity of statutes and regulations that you are dealing with, and the highly technical and complex nature of many of these requirements.

In-house and outside counsel should familiarize themselves with this complex area of the law in order to assist their clients in developing effective compliance programs tailored to their particular operations. Counsel also should understand the enforcement arsenal available to governmental authorities—and private citizens—as well as the basic tactics for preventing or minimizing the adverse impacts to the client if an enforcement action is brought. This chapter provides an overview of environmental law enforcement mechanisms, how governmental authorities set enforcement priorities and pursue them, and how practitioners can assist their clients in complying with environmental requirements and handling enforcement issues should they arise.

This chapter is not a primer on substantive environmental law—a topic that fills large sections of law libraries. Rather, the chapter seeks to give the practitioner a basic understanding of the enforcement framework in the environmental area, and some basic tips for handling enforcement matters. We have drawn on our experience in this field to create an overview of statutory enforcement authorities, governmental enforcement authorities, enforcement trends, and tips for avoiding or minimizing penalties. We hope to demystify this area of law and provide a useful guide for in-house and outside counsel who do not specialize in the environmental field.

Environmental Enforcement Authorities

Both federal and state environmental laws provide a powerful arsenal of enforcement tools, including civil fines that can be assessed in either administrative or judicial proceedings, criminal fines, injunctive relief (up to and including plant closure), and imprisonment of individuals for criminal violations. Criminal conviction under federal environmental laws can carry severe collateral consequences, including debarment from US government contracts. Most federal environmental statutes also include citizen suit provisions, which allow individuals or groups who can meet standing requirements to sue for penalties and injunctive relief.

A quick tour of the Clean Water Act penalty provisions shows the magnitude of the exposure for non-compliance. Civil penalties of up $25,000 per day may be imposed for violations of the Act or any permit condition or limitation established under the statute. The EPA may also seek temporary or permanent injunctions of conduct deemed to violate the Act. *See* 33 U.S.C. § 1319.

The Clean Water Act also provides for criminal penalties, and is exceptional in purporting to criminalize merely negligent conduct (as opposed to knowing or intentional conduct). The statute provides for misdemeanor penalties for certain negligent violations, including up to one year of imprisonment or up to a $25,000 fine per day of violation. Knowing violations are felonies punishable by up to three years of imprisonment or up to a $50,000 fine per day of violation. Violators who knowingly endanger another person are punishable by up to fifteen years of imprisonment and/or a fine up to $250,000. All of the foregoing penalties may be doubled if the violation is a repeat offense. In addition, a corporation that knowingly endangers a person by its violation of the Act may be subject to a fine of up to one million dollars. Individuals making false statements or tampering with monitoring devices related to the Clean Water Act may be subject to a fine up to $10,000 or up to two years imprisonment (fine and/or imprisonment may be doubled for repeat offenders). *See Id.*

Like other federal environmental statutes, the Clean Water Act authorizes private citizens to assume the enforcement role. The statute allows a private citizen (any individual or group meeting constitutional standing requirements) to bring suit against any person "who is alleged to be in violation of . . . an effluent standard or limitation" under the Act or any order issued by the EPA or a state regarding the standard or limitation. *See* 33 U.S.C. § 1365.

States have enacted their own comprehensive environmental statutes, which also provide for both civil and criminal penalties. In addition to their authority under their own statutes, states may assume from EPA primary regulatory and enforcement authority under federal environmental statutes. However, the federal government always retains the power to bring enforcement actions under federal environmental laws. Indeed, environmental law is unusual in that a single course of conduct may form the basis for both a federal *and* a state enforcement action. Moreover, governmental authorities may—and often do—bring both civil and criminal charges in cases involving wrongful conduct. As discussed in greater detail below, as defense counsel, you must ensure that your response to an action at one level does not leave your client open to enforcement at the other level for the same conduct.

Enforcement actions may be brought at the administrative agency level before an administrative law judge or in court. In collaboration with EPA, the US Department of Justice brings environmental criminal cases and the larger civil enforcement cases (i.e., those seeking large civil penalties and/or involving enforcement priorities as to which the government wants to "make a statement") in federal court. However, the majority of both federal and state enforcement activity occurs at the administrative agency level. It is therefore important for practitioners to understand the substantive and procedural differences between administrative and judicial enforcement actions—a topic further explored below.

It is also important to appreciate that inaccurate reporting to an environmental agency, or a failure to report an event that is required to be reported, may in and of itself lead to civil and criminal penalties. Environmental laws and regulations (as well as individual facility permits) generally have extensive monitoring, recordkeeping and reporting requirements and quite significant penalties may attach for incorrect, incomplete, or untimely reporting. Reporting violations are relatively easy for enforcement authorities to establish and it is quite common to see them in both administrative and judicial complaints. Moreover, in some cases, the government may bring enforcement action for reporting violations under both environmental law and general reporting statutes, particularly the federal False Claims Act.

Current Enforcement Priorities

Although an enforcement action may be brought for *any* alleged violation of an environmental statute, regulation or permit—and may seem to come out of the blue—you can assess the odds to some extent with a bit of knowledge about governmental enforcement priorities and trends. First, you should know that EPA has a formal planning process for setting its enforcement "priorities" on a three-year schedule. For the period including fiscal years 2011-2013, the Agency has established the following six enforcement "initiatives:"

1. Eliminating raw sewage and contaminated stormwater discharges from combined sewer overflows, sanitary sewer overflows, and municipal separate storm sewer systems.
2. Preventing waste from Concentrated Animal Feeding Operations from contaminating surface and ground waters.
3. Reducing emissions of hazardous air pollutants, particularly in local communities that are disproportionately impacted by pollution from multiple sources, focusing on leak detection and repair requirements, restrictions on flaring, excess emissions occurring during start-up, shutdown and malfunction events.
4. Enforcing new source review and prevention of significant deterioration requirements with a particular focus on large emission sources such as coal-fired power plants, refineries, cement manufacturing facilities, sulfuric and nitric acid manufacturing facilities, and glass manufacturing facilities.
5. Reducing water and air pollution from mining and mineral processing facilities and enforcing hazardous waste management and health and safety requirements applicable to mining and mineral processing facilities.
6. Assuring that energy extraction activities are complying with federal requirements to reduce or prevent pollution of air, water,

and land, with focus on particular areas of the country where energy extraction activities are concentrated.

See National Enforcement Initiatives, ETA.gov, http://www.epa.gov/compliance/data/planning/initiatives/index.html (last visited July 6, 2011). Clients with operations in these industry sectors clearly should be particularly vigilant in their compliance efforts.

The EPA solicits public comments on its enforcement priorities, which is a valuable opportunity for industry to provide input. Working with your client and/or its trade association to submit comments on EPA's proposed enforcement agenda is one avenue for helping to redirect enforcement attention away from your client's operations.

To some extent, a client's enforcement risk depends on the location of its operations. First, federal enforcement priorities differ by EPA region. Moreover, states have their own enforcement priorities based on their particular policy agendas and environmental concerns.

Enforcement priorities are not driven by EPA or state environmental agencies alone; elected officials can play an important role too. For example, we represent a number of clients in the energy sector, and there has been a great deal of interest in Congress recently around the issue of hydraulic fracturing to facilitate natural gas production. We can predict that there will be an increase in future enforcement activity regarding this practice, and it is likely to be driven by congressional committees that are now investigating the alleged adverse environmental impacts of this practice.

In addition, environmental groups have set their own enforcement and policy agendas, and these determine how the groups allocate resources for citizen suits. For example, in recent years, environmental advocates have sought to restrict mountaintop mining, which has led to a number of citizens' suits against mining companies.

Trends in Environmental Enforcement

Over the past five to ten years, enforcement of environmental laws has increasingly included a policymaking angle, with the EPA seeking to achieve through enforcement what it has not been able to accomplish through regulation. This is partly a result of the delays and the inevitable litigation that occur during the rulemaking process. For example, the EPA had expected that the regulatory programs established in the Clean Air Amendments of 1977 (such as the Prevention of Significant Deterioration and New Source Review programs) would result in either the installation of state-of-the-art pollution control systems on, or the retirement of, older, less efficient and uncontrolled coal-fired power plants. When this did not occur, the EPA made coal-fired power plants a major enforcement target, including cases against Cinergy, Duke Power, AEP, and Alabama Power. These cases have resulted in significant settlements that require the installation of controls and/or the shuttering of numerous aging coal-fired plants, thereby achieving the EPA's original regulatory policy goals.

We believe that the debates going on today in the context of Clean Air Act toxic pollutants and climate change rulemakings underscore the frustration that regulatory agencies and environmental groups are having with the inability to get state-of-the-art controls placed on significant sources of air pollution. In this atmosphere, we expect that the trend of the expanded role that enforcement is playing in environmental policy today will continue.

We expect to see continued emphasis on enforcement under the Clean Air Act for another reason as well. Air pollution regulatory standards are going to continue to get tighter, and states are going to have to develop more aggressive control programs—a situation that will give rise to more compliance obligations. Consequently, within the next five years or so, we are likely to see many more environmental enforcement cases brought under the Clean Air Act, whether they are brought by the EPA, the states, or by citizen groups.

We also anticipate that environmental public interest groups will continue bringing citizen suits under the major environmental statutes, including the Clean Air Act, Clean Water Act and the Resource Conservation Recovery Act. We believe that the increase in citizen suits in recent years reflects a frustration at the grassroots level, in that many citizens do not see the EPA or the state agencies as being aggressive enough in terms of environmental law enforcement. As federal and state governments encounter increasing budget pressures that could limit their own enforcement activity, citizen groups will seek to step into the breach.

Prevention Is Key

Environmental law is a field in which an ounce of prevention is worth a pound of cure. The most important step your client can take to avoid the imposition of penalties under environmental laws is to implement a strong environmental compliance program. The elements of the program will vary based on the nature of the client's business, but an effective program generally should include (1) clear and unwavering management support; (2) well-trained staff who are given the resources necessary to ensure compliance; (3) clear written policies and procedures for conducting environmentally sound and legally compliant operations, including regular inspection and maintenance of pollution control equipment and waste handling; (4) schedules and procedures for environmental sampling and monitoring; (5) reporting procedures—both internally and to regulatory authorities; (6) a process for investigating environmental incidents and implementing changes to prevent a recurrence; and (7) periodic compliance auditing coupled with a rigorous process for prompt resolution of deficiencies found in auditing.

Counsel can also facilitate their clients' compliance efforts by assisting them in the environmental permitting process. For example, counsel can work with regulatory agency permit writers and the client's business representatives and technical experts to ensure that permit requirements are clearly written, appropriately tailored to the client's actual operations, and practically achievable.

In order to assist clients in the compliance and permitting areas, you first need to know your client's business operations from top to bottom, and you need to know the relevant people within the company with whom you should be communicating. It is critical as you develop an environmental compliance management system that your client representative has the appropriate authority and responsibility to be able to assist you in developing an effective strategy. You need to know which of your client's business operations are subject to environmental law requirements, as well as the people who are involved with those operations.

Secondly, you need to understand the overall regulatory framework that applies to your client's operations. Whether your client has a sophisticated technical staff to help you or you need to hire environmental consultants to assist you, it is important to understand the framework for a compliance program that takes into consideration the requirements that apply to your client.

Next, you need to identify the manner in which you are going to designate the specific program elements to ensure compliance at each of the client's compliance points. For example, assume that your client is subject to five different environmental regulatory programs (which is not a stretch). In that case, the client needs to understand, in the context of each of those five regulatory schemes, what their specific obligations are in terms of permitting, compliance with the relevant standards, recordkeeping, monitoring, and reporting.

Once you have identified applicable requirements and understood their application to the client's operations, you should work with the client and its technical advisors to translate complex environmental regulations into practical, readily understood compliance procedures that line personnel will actually use. Impenetrable compliance manuals gathering dust on the shelf may well end up as a prosecutor's exhibit showing your client knew what it was supposed to do, but failed to do, under applicable environmental laws and regulations.

It is often said—and bears repeating—that the first and most important element of a successful compliance program is a firm commitment on the part of management to implement and maintain the program. Simply put, compliance is good business. In addition to demonstrating good corporate citizenship, consistent compliance avoids the substantial financial and reputational cost of an enforcement action. Moreover, effective pollution prevention and conservation programs can reduce the client's costs for raw materials and waste handling. Of course, corporate leaders have a personal stake in compliance as well. Under the doctrine of corporate officer liability, there is real individual exposure for noncompliance with environmental requirements.

You do not need to start from scratch in creating a compliance program. For example, your client's industry trade associations may have helpful guidance documents, checklists, audit protocols, and other materials that can give the client a good start. Industry organizations and trade groups can provide the opportunity for environmental professionals to benchmark their programs—for example, an environmental compliance manager can glean very useful information through inquiries to other, similarly situated professionals such as, "This is how I handled an inspection last week regarding Region 4. Does anybody else in the room have experience with what is going to happen next—and is there something that I can do differently next time as a result of what happened to our company this time?" It is helpful to either work with your client or get your client involved in such organizations in order to give them opportunities that will benefit the compliance system your client wants to put in place.

Where Enforcement Starts

We believe that one of the most important things that lawyers and their clients need to understand in the environmental enforcement arena is that enforcement actually starts with your first interaction with a regulatory agency, even if it is not with the enforcement staff. If you are dealing with a company whose facilities are subject to regulation, the first interaction they will typically have with a regulatory agency will create a compliance point for purposes of enforcement; and every step going forward also has compliance points. For example, when seeking to locate a facility in a certain area, a company will normally need to assess the need for air permits, wastewater permits, and a compliance system for hazardous waste management. These activities will involve communication with local and state, and sometimes federal, regulatory agencies responsible for these programs. Although these initial communications are not with enforcement staff, they will set the stage for the manner in which the facility is regulated, and will set the tone for the relationship with the regulatory agency. Therefore, when you are representing a company as outside or in-house environmental counsel, you need to make sure that your client understands that every decision made along the way has potential enforcement ramifications.

Another key point that should be made clear to the client is that *every* interaction with a government official or employee is an opportunity either to minimize or increase the risk of an enforcement action. For example, everyone knows (or should know) that a governmental inspection represents a potential for enforcement for any noncompliance that is discovered during the course of the inspection. Clients also need to understand that it presents an opportunity for the company to put forward its best face, demonstrate its commitment to compliance, and otherwise show the state or federal authorities that it takes compliance with environmental laws very seriously. In our experience, the manner in which an inspection is handled can steer an enforcement process in a direction that is favorable to the company or 180 degrees in the other direction—in which case, the company ends up being subject to a much more severe environmental enforcement action. Ensuring that your client understands this, and has in place a specific procedure for handling inspections in a proactive and professional manner, can go a long way toward ensuring a positive working relationship with the regulatory agencies, including enforcement staff in an enforcement scenario.

Differences in State and Federal Proceedings

Typically, an enforcement action at the state level can be a much less formal and more cooperative process than federal enforcement. These cases often can and should be resolved with in-house people. In fact, our experience is that we do not get many calls for assistance in those kinds of cases. We do have discussions regarding how to handle those types of cases with our long-term clients, but that is a very different discussion than a situation where we are asked to represent a major company that has just received a federal civil complaint, and the role of lead counsel is going to be much greater and quite different in that context.

Generally, the EPA has a number of civil enforcement and response policies that it applies in federal enforcement cases, regardless of the magnitude of the case. That is not always the case at the state level. Therefore, a client that is facing even a relatively minor noncompliance issue with the EPA needs to recognize that there are specific, formal procedures and a process that will be involved in negotiating resolution of the matter. For example, a company that is alleged to be in noncompliance with Clean Air Act requirements that apply to mobile sources will be proceeding down the path that is prescribed in the Agency's mobile source enforcement policy, regardless of the magnitude of the violation.

Conversely, in many cases the process at the state level is not going to be as formally prescribed, and there are going to be opportunities to get your case on a fast track to resolution through negotiation of an administrative penalty order or the like. At the state level, you are less likely to be boxed in by formal response policies as you would be when trying to resolve an issue under the EPA's civil penalty policies.

Responding to a Notice of an Environmental Violation at the Administrative Level

The process for responding to a notification of an environmental violation will differ from case to case, based on a number of factors. Such factors include whether the action is at the federal or state level, what statute your client is alleged to have violated, and the factual circumstances underlying the alleged noncompliance. The initial notification may be a notice of violation; if so, you will likely be given an opportunity to request a conference to discuss the notice and argue your case at the administrative level, without the formal trappings of a court case. Sometimes there is a step before receiving a notice of violation where the client will be contacted either formally or informally by an agency representative, who will say in effect, "We believe that there has been noncompliance on your part in regard to a certain action. Would you like to provide us with information that would result in us deciding otherwise?" Clients are well served to take advantage of any and all opportunities to make their best arguments prior to initiation of a formal enforcement action.

There are times when the magnitude of the environmental violation is significant enough that the agency believes that it does not have a choice with respect to taking the administrative route—for example, if the agency believes that the noncompliance posed a threat to human health or the environment, or was sufficiently serious to suggest a pattern of noncompliance. In that case, your client's first notice of a violation may be a receipt of a civil complaint; but that is the exception rather than the rule.

Fortunately, most of the environmental enforcement that we see is at the administrative level, whether it stems from a federal or state agency. The enforcement process is much less formal in the administrative context; and there are, in most cases, numerous opportunities to be able to resolve the environmental enforcement action before it gets to the level of a judicial complaint—and hopefully before it gets to the level of any spillover into a criminal proceeding.

In terms of the specific processes that are invoked, much depends on the statute or regulatory program that the company has allegedly violated (e.g., the Clean Air Act or Clean Water Act), and again whether you are dealing with a state or federal agency. Regardless of what process you are dealing with, it is critical that both the lawyer and the client, to the maximum extent possible, manage the process by working with the enforcement agency, because your opportunities to resolve an issue favorably increase exponentially if you are able to work with the enforcement team from the environmental agency that is seeking to enforce a particular regulation. Establishing your credibility early on in the process is essential to the success of the process; credibility once lost is very rarely, if ever, regained. Consequently, it is critical to ensure that information provided to the agency, whether in the context of responding to a formal information request, notice of violation, or otherwise, is 100 percent accurate.

Penalty Mitigation and Settlement Considerations

Fortunately, there are usually multiple opportunities to mitigate environmental noncompliance penalties. For example, the degree to which an entity cooperates in the context of an enforcement action can significantly mitigate the penalty imposed. Similarly, if the entity promptly reports noncompliance that it discovers, and promptly comes into compliance, a penalty may be further graded downward. Counsel should familiarize themselves with any penalty calculation factors that may be prescribed directly in the relevant environmental statute. Counsel should also consult the EPA's penalty policy for the statute upon which an enforcement action or investigation is predicated, as the policies discuss both mitigating and aggravating factors. Counsel should also be familiar with the EPA's audit policy ("Incentives for Self-Policing: Discovery, Disclosure, Correction and Prevention of Violations"), as well as state corollaries, that set forth criteria for mitigating, in some cases completely, penalties for noncompliance that is discovered and corrected in the context of an environmental audit, that is timely reported to the Agency, and that meets certain other criteria.

Most environmental enforcement proceedings are resolved through settlement, partly because the standard for imposing penalties is quite low (strict liability in the case of civil penalties) and because environmental statutes include very few affirmative defenses. But that is not to say that the client should rush to settlement, as it may well have viable defenses based on agency misinterpretation of a statute or regulation, statute of limitations, or technical deficiencies in the agency's evidence. Counsel should carefully evaluate each and every potential defense early in the case.

In resolving an enforcement matter through settlement, one of your principal goals should be to ensure that the settlement releases all potential claims associated with the conduct at issue. There may be multiple players and a variety of different claims involved in environmental cases, particularly in a larger enforcement action. Almost without exception, any environmental violation may potentially involve both federal and state claims and, if possible, you will want to resolve all of them in a single consent agreement.

One of the most important policy issues we have focused on over the past fifteen to twenty years has been the concept of over-filing, which refers to the federal government bringing its own enforcement action when the state has already commenced enforcement proceedings. You do not want to be in a situation where you negotiate a settlement with the state on favorable terms, but a federal agency that disagrees with how the state is proceeding or with the scope of the state settlement uses its federal authority to bring a federal action, whether administrative or civil judicial, predicated upon the exact same conduct. Accordingly, it is essential that you have all of the key actors at the table in order to negotiate a global settlement resolving *all* claims—federal and state, civil and criminal. Involving all of the stakeholders throughout the process—not just toward the end—is vital to achieving a comprehensive settlement.

A global settlement is especially important if your client is facing parallel criminal and civil proceedings. The government may seek to resolve the civil case first, leaving your client exposed on the criminal side because the factual findings in the civil enforcement action as a practical matter may establish the essential elements of the alleged environmental crime.

Helpful Resources

When we first started practicing environmental law, there were almost no published sources of information. These days, however, one can become overwhelmed with treatises, articles, newsletters, and other sources of information about environmental law. Fortunately, the EPA's own website is an excellent and readily accessible source of information. For someone who is not expert in the environmental area, the site has general descriptions of its regulatory programs that provide a good basic overview. The site also has links to the major federal environmental statutes and regulations and a trove of important agency policy and guidance documents. Once you have mastered the fundamentals, you will want to stay abreast of the regulatory and enforcement developments that are most important to your practice. We suggest that you determine the three or four most useful and practical sources that you are going to read on a weekly basis in order to stay up-to-date on developments.

You cannot take shortcuts when you are looking for the type of technical information you will need to rely on in order to advise your clients in this Google-enabled world. Environmental law practitioners should avoid thinking that the first answer that pops up when they do a Google search on compliance will provide the information they should use to advise their client. There is no substitute for making sure that the information you are relying on is accurate and current when you give advice to your client.

Particularly in a highly technical area such as the Clean Air Act, you will need a great deal of experience working with these issues to feel comfortable handling a complex counseling or enforcement matter. There are many different interpretive guidance documents and other materials that are not readily accessible on a website, and you will need to learn the Clean Air Act law, as well as the all-important "lore," in this highly specialized area to be effective as lead counsel. A similar example of this arises in another of our primary areas of practice—the Toxic Substances Control Act (TSCA). Under TSCA, which establishes requirements for reporting, recordkeeping, and testing requirements, and restrictions relating to the manufacture, importation or processing of chemical substances, there are many technical guidance materials that are not always easy to locate or to understand. If you find you are out of your depth, consult with experienced counsel and involve technical experts as needed.

Within our practice we have specialists in all of the major substantive areas of environmental law. At the same time, we require our lawyers to develop a strong command of all of the organic statutes and many of the major state environmental programs, because in our field everything truly is connected to everything else. For example, you may not be able to fully advise a client on a hazardous waste problem unless you understand what happens to the hazardous waste—i.e., is it emitted through a smokestack, in which case it may become a Clean Air Act issue; or does it settle on the ground, which may turn into a Superfund problem? This broad knowledge base is important in the enforcement context, particularly when representing clients with respect to "multimedia" inspections or enforcement actions, which the EPA conducts under multiple environmental statutes simultaneously.

Conclusion

The complexities of federal and state environmental laws, the multiple stakeholders involved in the enforcement of environmental laws, and the severe penalties prescribed for violating these laws all underscore the need for thorough preparation by environmental counselors and advocates in representing their clients. It is critical to understand the substantive and procedural requirements set forth in relevant federal and state laws, and to become familiar with the multiple venues in which environmental laws are enforced, and by whom.

Practitioners would also be well served to understand and, if appropriate, participate in the development of environmental enforcement priorities at the federal level, and to follow relevant trends in enforcement, whether they involve a national focus on specific industrial sectors or a regional or state focus on issues of special importance to the region or state.

Perhaps most importantly, environmental lawyers must know their clients' business operations inside and out, know how the myriad environmental requirements apply to these operations, and help the client develop and implement a proactive environmental compliance management system to lessen the chances that the client finds itself on the receiving end of an environmental enforcement action. For us, getting to know our clients and understanding their business is the most gratifying and interesting part of environmental practice.

Key Takeaways

- Knowing your client and your client's business will enable you to give the most effective advice on complying with the environmental laws. You also need to have a firm grasp of the regulatory frameworks under each of the major organic statutes, and work with your client to identify which regulations apply to their company or industry.
- Working constructively with the regulator—from the first point of contact—will facilitate the successful resolution of any enforcement issues that may arise. Establishing your credibility early on is also essential to the success of the process. Information provided to the agency has to be 100 percent accurate both to establish trust and to comply with statutory and regulatory reporting requirements.
- Make your clients understand that an environmental inspection is not only a potential issue for enforcement, but that it also presents an opportunity for the company. The manner in which an inspection is handled can steer an enforcement process in a direction that is favorable to the company, or the company may end up being subject to a much more severe environmental enforcement action.
- Determine the three or four most useful and practical sources that you are going to read on a weekly basis in order to stay up-to-date on developments in this area. There are many different interpretive guidance documents and other materials that are not readily accessible on a website. Therefore, when you start getting into technical compliance issues and the enforcement context in a particular area, you need to know the law in a way that very few people do.
- The best way to avoid a costly enforcement action is to help your client establish an effective compliance program and work with the client on periodic audits to assure continued compliance.

***Carol Clayton** is a partner in Wilmer Cutler Pickering Hale and Dorr LLP's Regulatory and Government Affairs Department, leader of the firm's Environmental Practice Group, and Partner in Charge of the firm's Washington, D.C. office. Ms. Clayton has practiced environmental law for more than twenty-five years, representing clients in the energy, manufacturing, chemicals, waste disposal, transportation, and financial services industries in a wide range of environmental counseling, litigation, and transactional matters. She has defended clients in a range of federal and state investigative and enforcement proceedings; she also handles private litigation among parties seeking to allocate liability for environmental response costs. Ms. Clayton assists clients with the development of environmental compliance and auditing programs, including voluntary audits performed under consent agreements in enforcement matters. She also represents clients in connection with the environmental permitting and NEPA review for major infrastructure projects. Ms. Clayton's practice spans the range of major federal and state environmental laws, and currently includes substantial federal Clean Water Act, Oil Pollution Act, and Clean Air Act matters.*

Ms. Clayton received her JD degree from the University of Virginia School of Law, where she was an editor of the Virginia Journal of Natural Resources Law. *The* National Law Journal *named Ms. Clayton as one of ten legal "Visionaries" and the* Washingtonian Magazine *named her one of the 100 Most Powerful Women in Washington in 2009.*

***Kenneth (Ken) Meade** is a partner in Wilmer Cutler Pickering Hale and Dorr LLP's Regulatory and Government Affairs Department, and a member of the Environmental, Public Policy and Strategy and Government Regulatory Litigation Practice Groups. His practice focuses on enforcement and counseling relating to federal and state environmental laws, Clean Air Act, and climate change permitting, counseling and enforcement, and counseling related to the development of natural resources. He has been actively involved in representing clients subject to civil and criminal investigations of federal and state environmental laws, including advising clients regarding the development, implementation and management of environmental management systems and internal environmental auditing programs and investigations, for more than twenty years, including serving as counsel to the Corporate Environmental Enforcement Council (CEEC), an organization of more than twenty companies from a wide range of industrial sectors that focuses exclusively on civil and criminal environmental enforcement public policy issues.*

Mr. Meade received his JD, with honors, from the National Law Center at the George Washington University and his BA in political science from the University of

Michigan. He was recognized as a leader in environmental law in the 2011 edition of Chambers USA: America's Leading Lawyers for Business.

Acknowledgement: *The authors wish to thank Bonnie Heiple, an environmental associate in Wilmer Hale's Boston office, for her valuable assistance in the preparation of this chapter.*

Surviving the Enforcement First Culture

Jeffrey R. Porter

Environmental Section Chairperson

Mintz Levin Cohn Ferris Glovsky and Popeo PC

ASPATORE

Introduction

The web of federal and state environmental laws and regulations has never been more complicated. At the same time, the government is unable or unwilling to provide comprehensive compliance assistance to the regulated community. This convergence of complex and sometimes inconsistent legal requirements and a government "enforcement first" strategy challenge the regulated community as it has never been challenged before.

This chapter discusses the root causes of the "enforcement first" approach to environmental compliance and how the regulated community can most effectively respond to the increasingly hostile regulatory environment this approach creates.

The Genesis of the Enforcement First Approach

There are, I think, four root causes of the government's enforcement first approach to compliance.

First, over the course of the modern environmental regulatory era, beginning in the mid-1970s, the government has had the benefit of very broad enabling statutes, giving it nearly unfettered discretion to promulgate even more favorable to the government regulations and policies. After these statutes and regulations were interpreted by the regulators themselves, those interpretations were reviewed by courts inclined to give the government the benefit of every doubt. Not surprisingly, this led to the development of a precedent that further emboldened the government. One of the best examples of this phenomenon is in the Superfund arena in which a "polluter pays" doctrine evolved that, at its apex, emboldened the pursuit of "generators" of anything containing "hazardous substances" as broadly defined. *See, e.g.*, *US v. Burlington N. & Santa Fe Ry. Co.*, 520 F. 3d 918, 941 (9th Cir. 2007), rev'd; 129 S. Ct. 1870 (2009) ("At the liability stage, CERCLA simply assigns liability to statutorily responsible parties so as to assure that, as between those with some connection to the contamination—and who have, it may be assumed, benefited from the contamination-causing process—and those with none, such as the taxpayers.").

Second, many environmental regulators have had their budgets slashed. Perhaps because the regulatory agencies perceived it would cause the regulated community to advocate for additional funds for the regulators, or perhaps because regulators determined that enforcement provides a "bigger bang for the buck," compliance assistance has been reduced and "compliance monitoring" has continued. In fiscal year 2010, the EPA conducted 21,000 inspections. More than one in four of those inspections identified a "potential violation." [1]

Third, the economic recession has made the regulated community less popular while the "green" movement has heightened environmental sensitivity. This has emboldened regulators to more aggressively pursue an enforcement first approach.

The fourth and final cause of the enforcement first approach is the perceived inability of elected and appointed managers of many regulatory agencies to manage in the way private sector managers do. I think the reasons for this include the fact that elected and appointed managers of environmental agencies are, for the most part, unable to hire and fire their subordinates and, as a result, subordinates are able to "outlast" their elected and appointed managers. In addition, the subject matter of enforcement proceedings is often sufficiently complicated that it is impossible for elected and appointed mangers of regulatory agencies to sufficiently understand the details of those proceedings in a way that allows them to challenge staff even if they were inclined to do so.

These four factors have collectively resulted in the expansion of what I refer to as the enforcement "bubble." However, like most bubbles it can expand only so much.

That brings me to the most significant force opposing the continued inflation of the enforcement bubble— the rejection of the liberal reading of environmental statutes by the judiciary. In *Burlington Northern*, the Supreme Court insisted that proof of an arrangement for disposal requires

[1] *Compliance and Enforcement Annual Results 2010 Fiscal Year*, EPA.GOV, http://www.epa.gov/compliance/resources/reports/endofyear/eoy2010/index.html (last visited July 6, 2011).

proof of an intention to effect a disposal (as defined by the statute). 129 S.Ct. 1870, 1879-80 (2009). In June 2011, the Supreme Court granted a petition for a writ of certiorari to answer the question of whether the homeowner recipients of an EPA administrative order to demolish their house could seek pre-enforcement judicial review of that order and, if they can't, whether the order violates their constitutional due process rights. *Sackett v. EPA*, No. 10-1062, 2011 WL 675769 (U.S. June 28, 2011). We have not yet begun to see the effect of these judicial actions in the government's decisions about which cases to enforce and how to enforce them.

In any event, clients are unlikely to think that resort to the Supreme Court is a successful strategy for most cases. Therefore, other successful strategies for operating in an enforcement first environment are the subject of the remainder of this chapter.

Agencies Participating in Environmental Law Enforcement

The primary federal agency involved in environmental law enforcement is, of course, the Environmental Protection Agency (EPA). The EPA operates through its headquarters in Washington, D.C. and ten regional offices around the country. There is often not as much uniformity as one might expect in how the same laws and regulations are enforced by the different EPA regional offices. This requires one to understand and account for differences in positions among regions and to know, or find out, how the EPA headquarters might address such a difference in a given case.

Obviously, there may be a price to be paid in complaining to EPA headquarters about a decision in a regional office. The regional office will, of course, defend its position and will have access to the decision makers at headquarters that is likely to be better than yours. Therefore, this is not a decision to be made lightly. The best strategy will be one that is attuned to potential differences between a regional office view and what headquarters might require, and an early concerted effort to communicate with the regional office about the flexibility it may have, but not be exercising. Even if one is unsuccessful at the regional level, the record of the attempt to bridge a gap early will be important in any future conversation with headquarters.

Each state typically has some version of the EPA. For example, in Massachusetts, where I live, that agency is the Department of Environmental Protection. State agencies have the primary responsibility for enforcing state laws and regulations that may be the same as or different from the federal laws and regulations (or laws and regulations of other states) dealing with the same topic. There are countless examples of this phenomenon. One straightforward example is that the federal Superfund statute's definition of "hazardous substances" specifically excludes petroleum while the Massachusetts analog includes both "oil" and "hazardous materials."[2]

There is a wide spectrum of flexibility and responsiveness among state environmental agencies, and even among divisions of state environmental agencies. What may be a very reasonable request in one state may be out of the question in another state.

The state agencies also have primary responsibility for enforcing federal laws and regulations where responsibility for those programs has been delegated to the state.

Other Key Players in Environmental Law Enforcement

The Department of Justice (DOJ) and the State Attorneys General are critically important players in environmental law enforcement.

There is an entire division of the Department of Justice, the Environment and Natural Resources Division, that is responsible for enforcing more than one hundred federal laws. It has offices in six cities in addition to Washington, D.C.

In each United States Attorney's office there is also at least one assistant United States attorney who works with EPA's lawyers to represent the regional EPA office in litigation.

---

[2] Compare definition of "hazardous substances" in the Comprehensive Environmental Response, Compensation and Liability Act found at 42 U.S.C. §9601(14) and the definition of "oil" in the Massachusetts Oil and Hazardous Material Release Prevention and Response Act, M.G.L. 21E § 2.

I have found that the interaction between EPA and the DOJ is somewhat equivalent to the interaction between an in-house lawyer of a corporation and an outside lawyer for that corporation. Even if EPA lawyers have not responded to a particular argument, one might find the DOJ lawyer representing the EPA responsive because it is the DOJ lawyer who needs to prosecute or defend EPA's position in court. Having said that, you should expect a DOJ lawyer to break ranks with their EPA counterpart about as often as you would expect outside counsel to break ranks with the in-house lawyer of their client.

Many state environmental agencies also have staff lawyers who may work with lawyers from the office of the state attorney general in the same way that EPA and DOJ lawyers work together. Other state environmental agencies rely exclusively on the office of the state attorney general for this support.

The Role of Elected Officials in Environmental Law Enforcement Proceedings

Clients need to know that the regulatory agencies they are dealing with can be responsive to political forces. Often lawyers and clients do not appreciate how elected officials can positively or negatively affect how a regulatory agency approaches a particular issue.

We see this playing out in Washington, D.C. today in a very high profile matter. As you no doubt know, several states sued the EPA over its failure to regulate greenhouse gas emissions under the federal Clean Air Act. *Massachusetts v. EPA*, 127 S.Ct. 1438 (2007). The Supreme Court, siding with the states, determined that EPA was, in fact, required by the Clean Air Act to regulate greenhouse gas emissions. When EPA attempted to follow the Supreme Court's edict, members of Congress attempted to use the legislative process to neutralize the Supreme Court's decision. While no such legislation has passed, EPA has certainly responded to the forces behind such legislation by proceeding more "deliberately" and regulations that EPA has promulgated are the subject of judicial challenges by states.

Now I don't mean to suggest that many matters will garner the interest among elected officials that federal regulation of greenhouse gas emissions has attracted. However, it is a striking example of the power of political forces in environmental matters, even environmental matters that have been litigated to a conclusion. These forces can operate at any level of government from the federal government in Washington, D.C. to the local city council. Whether or not you intend to attempt to employ these forces, it is critically important to understand how they may be employed, and by whom, as you develop your strategy for a matter.

The Role of Outside Counsel in Environmental Compliance

Many of my clients now have an internal team dedicated to environmental law compliance and those internal teams are assisted by consultants with special expertise in specific areas. Those clients are much more sophisticated about environmental law compliance than the regulated industry was at the beginning of my career.

These clients are also much more focused about what they're looking for from their environmental counsel. They already have, either on their internal teams, or through their consultants, much of the know-how that they would have historically looked to their lawyer to provide.

Of course, other clients don't have these internal and external resources.

We owe it to all of our clients, regardless of their expertise and resources, to be as expert as we can be about the current federal and state requirements in the areas in which we practice, and to know as much as we can about how the relevant federal and state agencies are enforcing those requirements. We also owe it to our clients, and ourselves, to be in a position to add value in as many areas as possible and to be honest about those areas in which we don't. In today's sophisticated market, our clients are likely to figure that out quickly in any event.

Even a very sophisticated client may not have sufficient reason to know how state regulators are interpreting their regulations in a specific area. By remaining active in local bar and industry groups, good environmental counsel in that jurisdiction can provide specialized knowledge that may not otherwise be available, even from leading national environmental legal practices or engineering firms. For example, there is considerable variability in how EPA and various states are currently addressing the possibility that chemicals historically released to soil and groundwater might affect the quality of air inside buildings in the vicinity of those releases. In some cases, not even agency guidance has caught up with the current approach of agency staff. Only a lawyer or consultant who regularly deals with that staff will be able to provide effective counsel on this topic.

On the other hand, another environmental lawyer might be far better suited to advise the same client regarding the application of a specific federal regulation across several jurisdictions.

For instance, National Pollutant Discharge Elimination System (NPDES) permit writers are increasingly unlikely to solicit input from permit holders in the course of preparing a draft discharge permit, instead consulting a manual to identify the theoretical limits that they think a company should be able to achieve in its discharge. The limits that the permit writer would make enforceable in a permit are often completely divorced from the reality of the permit holder's operations, discharge, and the permit limits under which the permit holder is currently operating. In the absence of a proactive approach, the permit holder might not learn of its would-be limits until the permit is issued in draft form. A good practitioner in this area will know the regulator's general predilections and will engage in an early dialogue with the client and its consultants about what the client can achieve, help the client compare what it thinks it can achieve with what a draft permit is likely to require, and help the client assess ways that it may bridge the gap between those two things. These evaluations can be very time and resource intensive for the client and may require additional external resources. However, only after such an evaluation will a client be prepared to approach the agency to advocate in favor of something other than what the agency may initially have in mind.

Understanding Your Client's Operations

The old cliché about "an ounce of prevention being worth a pound of cure" is particularly true about environmental compliance. Because "[p]rosecution remains a cornerstone of [the government's] integrated approach to ensure broad-based environmental compliance,"[3] and, as indicated above, more than one in every four government inspections reveals a potential violation, there is no substitute for an effective compliance plan. However, before you can provide meaningful assistance to your client in developing an effective compliance plan, you need to understand your client's operations. Your client may be able to provide you with the basis of this understanding. This may also involve the services of appropriate consultants working with the client to evaluate their operations.

Once you sufficiently understand your client's operations and you have identified the federal, state, and local statutes and regulations that apply to them, you will be in a position to work with your client to distill that understanding into a compliance plan that is easy to implement. It is critically important that the compliance plan be periodically re-evaluated to ensure that it is up to date.

Frankly, a compliance plan that is not sufficiently understandable to all of the people who need to understand it, or is not up to date, can be worse than not having a plan at all because regulators might use the plan as evidence against your client. Comparing the elements of a compliance plan to conduct at a facility that conflicts with the elements of that plan can make a regulator's job of establishing a violation easy.

Addition by Subtraction

I have found that many clients do not pay sufficient attention to the possibility of "addition by subtraction." For example, there may be process changes that would change the nature or volume of an emission to eliminate or at least reduce a client's regulatory burden. There can be no more efficient response to complex regulations than to develop a response that takes your client out of a regulatory "game" entirely, or at least out of the "big leagues." That is why sophisticated clients and their lawyers will increase their attention to opportunities to minimize the regulatory "footprint" of their operations while at the same time ensuring that the requirements to which they are still subject are as easy to understand as

[3] See U.S. DEP'T OF JUSTICE, STEWARDS OF THE AMERICAN DREAM, FY 2007-FY 2012 STRATEGIC PLAN, 63.

possible for the people actually involved in the operations that are subject to those requirements.

Compliance Training and Documentation

Once your client has minimized its regulatory footprint to the greatest degree possible, the next challenge is to make the remaining regulatory requirements as accessible as possible to everyone involved in the operations affected by those regulations. In other words, it is not sufficient for a client's in-house counsel to understand the plan. This means, among other things, clearly drawn lines regarding who is supposed to do what.

It also means taking the complicated issues we deal with and making them simple enough so that everybody can understand the pieces they need to understand. In my experience, one of the most common causes of environmental enforcement proceedings is that applicable requirements were not sufficiently digested for all of the people to whom the requirements were relevant.

An operator can be given a form that is specially designed for him to quickly, easily, and competently provide the information he is uniquely situated to provide that then finds its way into a much more complicated report required by the applicable regulations that is prepared by someone else. This minimizes the risk that the operator will ignore the form altogether or complete it inaccurately.

Giving sufficient thought to the documentation of environmental compliance is one of the best ways to avoid or at least quickly resolve an environmental enforcement proceeding.

Client Perspectives about Environmental Enforcement

I have found that there is a broad spectrum of respect for, or even fear of, governmental authority among clients faced with environmental law enforcement proceedings. At one end of that spectrum are those clients who react to word that they are the subject of such proceedings with the immediate reaction that they are innocent and will spare no expense to vindicate themselves. I've heard many clients say that "we are going to fight this proceeding to our dying breath." Fewer clients have actually done so. At the other end of the spectrum are those clients who assume that because the government tells them to do something, they must immediately do whatever it is that the government is demanding of them.

Of course, most often neither of these reactions is the right one. It is true that the role of the government in environmental law enforcement is unique because of its administrative authority. Essentially, the government is often—at least in the first instance—both the prosecutor and the judge. Many environmental statutes and regulations provide the regulator, whether it is the EPA or a state agency, with the choice of either commencing an enforcement proceeding in the courts or pursuing a violation administratively. If the agency itself issues an order requiring you to do or not do something, and/or administratively attempts to collect a penalty or otherwise require a payment, and you're unhappy with the agency's suggestion, you have to go through whatever procedures are specified by the agency to complain about the decision and then, and only then can you get limited judicial review by a court.

Therefore, an environmental law enforcement proceeding may be quite different from a typical litigation matter where allegations are adjudicated by a judge who at least theoretically does not have an affinity for either side.

I counsel my clients that the strategy for such matters depends on the specific circumstances of each case.

There are some cases in which we will decide that the best way to proceed is to attempt to reach closure as early as possible with as little process as possible either because the exposure to the client does not demand more, or because even if more was done one would be unlikely to get a significantly better result. Making this decision requires, among other things, a thorough understanding of the range of potential resolutions in such circumstances and an equally thorough understanding of the potential future implications of the resolution (i.e. does settlement require an agreement respecting future stipulated penalties or trigger heightened "repeat offender" sanctions?).

On the other hand, there are cases in which we know that an early resolution is impossible. This is most likely when there is a material disagreement about the facts at issue or the penalty sought for an alleged violation.

Responding to an Inspection

Any visit from a regulatory agency should be taken seriously. Hopefully your client is operating pursuant to a comprehensive, easy to understand and document, compliance plan when such a visit happens. Even if that's the case, your client should use the occasion of such an inspection to carefully assess what the inspectors may have seen. In some cases, you may be able to identify items that can be rectified in advance of any notice of noncompliance and being able to respond to such a notice that such items have already been addressed can mitigate a penalty the regulatory agency might otherwise seek.

Responding to a Notice of an Enforcement Proceeding

Needless to say, if your client has not already investigated the matters that are the subject of a notice of an enforcement proceeding (i.e. in connection with an agency inspection), it should do so upon learning of an enforcement proceeding against it. Counsel should speak to those who appear to be implicated and, at the same time, assemble and preserve any documents that relate to the subject of the notice. Fortunately, many clients have regular document retention policies. Upon receipt of notice of an enforcement proceeding, a client should ensure that such a policy does not result in the inadvertent destruction of relevant documents.

In the course of these early activities, you might determine that there are individuals or other entities that should have their own counsel because their interests might diverge from those of your client. That should happen quickly. You should also consider with your client whether you should suggest specific counsel to such individuals and entities and whether a joint defense agreement is appropriate. If a joint defense agreement might be appropriate, it should be negotiated as soon as possible.

Your client might have a knee jerk reaction to sever its relationship with an individual or an entity because of its receipt of notice of an enforcement proceeding. Whether this is in your client's best interests is something to be carefully considered.

Some lawyers would say that whenever enforcement is threatened, related communications should always be between lawyers. I disagree. I think many clients have the sophistication necessary to be able to deal directly with regulators, even in an enforcement context. In fact, I think there can be an advantage to a non-lawyer reaching out in certain circumstances because it results in more positive and productive conversations than might occur between lawyers. Of course, this depends on the specific circumstances of a matter, including the capabilities of the client, the regulator, and the complexity of the alleged violation and decisions in this regard should be made only after the initial investigations discussed above.

Ideally, before any communications with a regulatory agency, your client and you will have considered a range of acceptable outcomes arising from a notice of an enforcement proceeding. If, for example, based on your initial investigation, you and your client reasonably believe that the matter is susceptible of a quick resolution (for example technical non-compliance with a requirement that can likely be resolved by compliance and perhaps a modest penalty), that may suggest an initially informal and conciliatory response by the client directly to the regulator. If, on the other hand, it is clear that a matter is unlikely to be resolved quickly, or without high level involvement within the regulatory agency, that may suggest a different sort of response.

In any event, a free flowing exchange between the client and the regulator is unlikely to be the right answer. The substance of any communication directly between the client and the regulator should be carefully vetted in advance and the client should be counseled to remain true to the plan developed.

Criminal Sanctions in Environmental Law Enforcement Cases

Many federal and state environmental agencies now have law enforcement officers. The EPA is just one example of an agency with a police force. It is increasingly common for regulatory agencies to seek criminal sanctions for alleged environmental law violations. For decades, the government used civil enforcement to establish helpful precedents and it now uses those precedents in the criminal context.

However, the government has learned that criminal prosecutions present unique challenges that do not loom as large in the civil context. In criminal prosecutions, statutes and regulations are typically construed much more narrowly. Statutes and regulations that may pass muster in the civil arena may be confusing to a jury, or even to a trial court judge. The government is also faced with the constitutional protections against self-incrimination and in favor of full disclosure of evidence. In such cases it is, of course, critically important that competent criminal defense counsel work side by side with environmental counsel from the first hint of a criminal investigation.

The Role of Third Party Audits

Over the past decade, the government has often required third party compliance audits in the context of resolving enforcement proceedings. This requires the regulated entity to retain a third party consultant to periodically audit the compliance of the regulated entity with respect to any of a wide range of regulations including relating to air emissions, water discharges, and hazardous waste storage and disposal issues. The consultant then reports to the government and the regulated entity about the regulated entity's compliance. Any instances of non-compliance are typically subject to significant and escalating stipulated financial penalties.

Such third party compliance audits can be very expensive to implement. For this reason the scope and duration of such audits should be carefully considered.

Assisting Clients with Operations across the US and the World

If you have a client with similar operations in several jurisdictions, there may be significant differences with respect to the environmental regulations and enforcement practices in each of those jurisdictions and unfortunately, there is no shortcut to understanding those differences and making sure that your compliance plan reflects those differences.

This is another area in which the role of consultants has exploded over the past ten to fifteen years. If you have a client with regulatory issues in several jurisdictions and they do not have the necessary cross-jurisdiction expertise internally, you may need to help that client determine whether there is a role for a consultant, or consultants, to offer assistance in this regard.

Federal regulators are particularly interested in the circumstances of non-compliance in multiple jurisdictions.

Clients with international operations face an even greater challenge. Again, they need local experts familiar with each jurisdiction. If your client does not have the expertise to select such experts, you need to be honest about how your legal team can meet the needs of the client in each jurisdiction where the client may have issues.

Areas of Increased Enforcement Focus

Looking ahead, I think there will be an increasing focus on enforcement and increasing standardization in the government's approach. I also think that we will see an increasing focus on the prohibition of the use of certain chemicals perceived to be toxic or at least stronger regulations relating to the use and recycling of those materials.

I also think we will see an increased focus on the quality of indoor air. For most of my career indoor air standards have been the responsibility of the Occupational Safety and Health Administration (OSHA), and if indoor air concentrations of chemicals that were the subject of those standards were less than those OSHA levels that was good enough. There is, however, an increased focus by both state and federal governments on whether those OSHA levels are sufficiently protective, and whether enhanced remedial actions are required to prevent chemicals present in the environment from intruding into indoor spaces.

Another issue receiving increased attention is lead in paint in multi-family residential structures. Improper renovation and demolition of buildings containing asbestos also continues to be a focus of enforcement.

Conclusion

The "enforcement first" atmosphere is highly charged. Our clients face daunting regulatory requirements and stiff sanctions for not meeting those requirements. Thorough knowledge of the statutes, regulations, and case law in the jurisdictions in which we practice is essential to our success. However, that's just the beginning. We also need to know the regulators and how they interpret these sources of their authority so that we can counsel our clients on the best way to ensure compliance with those statutes and regulations, and how to most effectively interact with those interested in that compliance. Because the best way to do these things will vary case by case, there is no substitute for experience in this area.

Key Takeaways

- Environmental laws, regulations, and, until recently, case law are, for the most part, stacked against our clients. For this reason, among others, the "enforcement first" culture is likely to persist for the foreseeable future.
- An ounce of prevention is worth a pound of cure. There is no substitute for a comprehensive compliance plan that is easy to understand and implement at all levels of your client's organization.
- It is impossible to develop a good compliance plan without a thorough understanding of your client's operations and the statutes and regulations affecting those operations. This will require close coordination between your client, its consultants, and you.
- Effectively interacting with regulators before, during, and after initiation of enforcement proceedings requires knowledge of the regulator's predilections and practices that only comes with experience.

Jeffrey R. Porter has been recognized as one of the leading environmental lawyers in the United States by The Best Lawyers in America, Chambers USA: America's Leading Lawyers for Business, Who's Who in American Law, Who's Who in the World, Who's Who in America, *and the* Guide to the World's Leading Environmental Lawyers. *He is the author of countless articles and guest columns, and a commentator in numerous publications, including the* Wall Street Journal, Boston Business Journal, Banker and Tradesman, Massachusetts Lawyers Weekly, and the New England Real Estate Journal.

For almost twenty-three years, Mr. Porter has advised clients regarding complex environmental regulatory compliance and permitting issues. He received his BA, cum laude, *from Bates College and his JD from Cornell University.*

Acknowledgement: *I am grateful for the valuable contributions to this chapter by Colin Van Dyke, an associate in Mintz Levin's environmental law section. I am privileged to serve stellar clients and to be surrounded by many excellent environmental lawyers at Mintz Levin. However, the opinions presented in this chapter should not be attributed to any of them.*

Appendices

Appendix A

ADMINISTRATIVE CIVIL PENALTY CHART

Table of Selected EPA Administrative Civil Penalty Authority Limitations

Statute / Regulatory Program	Administrative Enforcement Limits	Citation
Clean Air Act		
Stationary Source Administrative Orders	$37,500 per day of violation and $295,000 maximum per order	42 U.S.C. § 7413(d)(1)
Mobile Sources	$295,000 maximum per order	42 U.S.C. § 7524(c)
Clean Water Act		
NPDES Permit and Wetland Related Penalties		
Class I Administrative Penalties	$16,000 per day of violation and maximum $37,500 per order	33 U.S.C. § 1319(g)(2)(A)
Class II Administrative Penalties	$16,000 per day of violation and maximum of $177,500 per order	33 U.S.C. § 1319(g)(2)(B)
Oil / Hazardous Substance Discharge Related Penalties		

Class I Administrative Penalties	$16,000 per day of violation and maximum $37,500 per order	33 U.S.C. § 1321(b)(6)(B)(i)
Class II Administrative Penalties	$16,000 per day of violation and maximum of $177,500 per order	33 U.S.C. § 1321(b)(6)(B)(ii)
Resource Conservation and Recovery Act		
Hazardous Waste Related Penalties	$37,500 per day per violation; no total limit on penalty amount in an order	42 U.S.C. §§ 6928(a)(3); 6928(c); 6928(h)(2)
Underground Storage Tank Related Penalties		
Failure to obey a compliance order	$37,500 per day of noncompliance	42 U.S.C. § 6991e(a)(3)
Failure to comply with technical requirements for USTs	$16,000 per tank for each day of noncompliance	42 U.S.C. § 6991e(d)(1)
Federal Insecticide Fungicide and Rodenticide Act		
Registrants	$7,500 per violation	7 U.S.C. § 136*l*(a)(1)
Private Applicators	$750 for first violation and $1,100 for each subsequent violation	7 U.S.C. § 136*l*(a)(2)

Toxic Substances Control Act	$37,500 per day per violation	15 U.S.C. § 2615(a)
Emergency Planning and Community Right to Know Act		
Failure to Obey a Compliance Order	$37,500 per day of violation	42 U.S.C. § 11045(a)
Class I Administrative Penalties re Failure to Notify EPA of a Release of Hazardous Substances	$37,500 per violation	42 U.S.C. § 11045(b)(1)
Class II Administrative Penalties re:		
• *Continuing Failures to Notify EPA of a Release*	$37,500 per day of continuing failure to report	42 U.S.C. § 11045(b)(2)
• *Repeat Violations of Release Reporting Requirements*	$107,500 per day in which repeat violation continues	42 U.S.C. § 11045(b)(2)
Tier II Reporting and Toxic Release Inventory Reporting	$37,500 per day per violation	42 U.S.C. § 11045(c)(1)
Submission of MSDSs and Health-Related Information	$16,000 per day per violation	42 U.S.C. § 11045(c)(2)
Frivolous Claims of Trade Secrets in EPCRA Submissions	$37,500 per claim	42 U.S.C. § 11045(d)

Courtesy of Sean M. Sullivan, Williams Mullen

Appendix B

CHEVRON, U.S.A., INC. V. NATURAL RESOURCES DEFENSE COUNCIL

Supreme Court of the United States
CHEVRON, U.S.A., INC., Petitioner,
v.
NATURAL RESOURCES DEFENSE COUNCIL, INC., et al.
AMERICAN IRON AND STEEL INSTITUTE, et al., Petitioners,
v.
NATURAL RESOURCES DEFENSE COUNCIL, INC., et al.
William D. RUCKELSHAUS, Administrator, Environmental Protection Agency, Petitioner,
v.
NATURAL RESOURCES DEFENSE COUNCIL, INC., et al.[FN*]

FN* US Reports Title: Chevron U.S.A. Inc. v. Natural Resources Defense Council, Inc.

Nos. 82-1005, 82-1247 and 82-1591.
Argued Feb. 29, 1984.
Decided June 25, 1984.

Rehearing Denied Aug. 16, 1984.

See 468 U.S. 1227, 105 S.Ct. 28, 29.

Petition was filed for review of order of the Environmental Protection Agency. The Court of Appeals, 685 F.2d 718, vacated regulations, and certiorari was granted. The Supreme Court, Justice Stevens, held that Environmental Protection Agency regulation allowing states to treat all pollution-emitting devices within same industrial grouping as though they were encased within single "bubble" was based on permissible construction of term "stationary source" in Clean Air Act Amendments.

Reversed.

West Headnotes

[1] Federal Courts 170B ⚷445

170B Federal Courts
170BVII Supreme Court
170BVII(A) In General
170Bk445 k. Appellate Jurisdiction and Procedure in General. Most Cited Cases

Supreme Court reviews judgments, not opinions.

[2] Statutes 361 ⚷219(2)

361 Statutes
361VI Construction and Operation
361VI(A) General Rules of Construction
361k213 Extrinsic Aids to Construction
361k219 Executive Construction
361k219(2) k. Existence of Ambiguity. Most Cited Cases

Statutes 361 ⚷219(4)

361 Statutes
361VI Construction and Operation
361VI(A) General Rules of Construction
361k213 Extrinsic Aids to Construction
361k219 Executive Construction
361k219(4) k. Erroneous Construction; Conflict with Statute. Most Cited Cases

When court reviews agency's construction of statute which it administers, court is confronted with two questions: whether Congress has directly spoken on precise question at issue; if statute is silent or ambiguous with respect to specific issue, question for court is whether agency's answer is based on permissible construction of statute.

[3] Statutes 361 ⚷219(4)

361 Statutes
361VI Construction and Operation
361VI(A) General Rules of Construction
361k213 Extrinsic Aids to Construction
361k219 Executive Construction
361k219(4) k. Erroneous Construction; Conflict with Statute. Most Cited Cases

Judiciary is final authority on issues of statutory construction and must reject administrative constructions which are contrary to clear congressional intent.

[4] Statutes 361 ⚷219(1)

361 Statutes
361VI Construction and Operation
361VI(A) General Rules of Construction
361k213 Extrinsic Aids to Construction
361k219 Executive Construction
361k219(1) k. In General. Most Cited Cases

Court need not conclude that agency's construction of statute which it administered was only one it permissibly could have adopted to uphold construction, or even reading the court would have reached if question initially had arisen in judicial proceeding.

[5] Statutes 361 ⚷219(1)

361 Statutes
361VI Construction and Operation
361VI(A) General Rules of Construction
361k213 Extrinsic Aids to Construction
361k219 Executive Construction
361k219(1) k. In General. Most Cited Cases

Where legislative delegation to agency on particular question is implicit rather than explicit, court may not substitute its own construction of statutory provision for reasonable interpretation made by administrator of agency.

[6] Statutes 361 ⚿219(1)

361 Statutes
361VI Construction and Operation
361VI(A) General Rules of Construction
361k213 Extrinsic Aids to Construction
361k219 Executive Construction
361k219(1) k. In General. Most Cited Cases

Considerable weight should be accorded to executive department's construction of statutory scheme it is entrusted to administer.

[7] Environmental Law 149E ⚿268

149E Environmental Law
149EVI Air Pollution
149Ek266 Particular Sources of Pollution
149Ek268 k. Stationary Sources in General. Most Cited Cases
(Formerly 199k25.6(3.1), 199k25.6(3) Health and Environment)

Environmental Protection Agency regulation allowing states to treat all pollution-emitting devices within same industrial grouping as though they were encased within single "bubble" was based on permissible construction of term "stationary source" in Clean Air Act Amendments. Clean Air Act, §§ 111(a)(3), 172(b)(6), 302(j), as amended, 42 U.S.C.A. §§ 7411(a)(3), 7502(b)(6), 7602(j).

Syllabus [FNa1]

FNa1. The syllabus constitutes no part of the opinion of the Court but has been prepared by the Reporter of Decisions for the convenience of the reader. See United States v. Detroit Lumber Co., 200 U.S. 321, 337, 26 S.Ct. 282, 287, 50 L.Ed. 499.

The Clean Air Act Amendments of 1977 impose certain requirements on States ****2779** that have not achieved the national air quality standards established by the Environmental Protection Agency (EPA) pursuant to earlier legislation, including the requirement that such "nonattainment" States establish a permit program regulating "new or modified major stationary sources" of air pollution. Generally, a permit may not be issued for such sources unless stringent conditions are met. EPA regulations promulgated in 1981 to implement the permit requirement allow a State to adopt a plantwide definition of the term "stationary source," under which an existing plant that contains several pollution-emitting devices may install or modify one piece of equipment without meeting the permit conditions if the alteration will not increase the total emissions from the plant, thus allowing a State to treat all of the pollution-emitting devices within the same industrial grouping as though they were encased within a single "bubble." Respondents filed a petition for review in the Court of Appeals, which set aside the regulations embodying the "bubble concept" as contrary to law. Although recognizing that the amended Clean Air Act does not explicitly define what Congress envisioned as a "stationary source" to which the permit program should apply, and that the issue was not squarely addressed in the legislative history, the court concluded that, in view of the purpose of the nonattainment program to improve rather than merely maintain air quality, a plantwide definition was "inappropriate," while stating it was mandatory in programs designed to maintain existing air quality.

Held: The EPA's plantwide definition is a permissible construction of the statutory term "stationary source." Pp. 2781–2793.

(a) With regard to judicial review of an agency's construction of the statute which it administers, if Congress has not directly spoken to the precise question at issue, the question for the court is whether the ***838** agency's answer is based on a permissible construction of the statute. Pp. 2781–2783.

(b) Examination of the legislation and its history supports the Court of Appeals' conclusion that Congress did not have a specific intention as to the applicability of the "bubble concept" in these cases. Pp. 2783–2786.

(c) The legislative history of the portion of the 1977 Amendments dealing with nonattainment areas plainly discloses that in the permit program Congress sought to accommodate the conflict between the economic interest in permitting capital improvements to continue and the environmental interest in improving air quality. Pp. 2786–2787.

(d) Prior to the 1977 Amendments, the EPA had used a plantwide definition of the term "source," but in 1980 the EPA ultimately adopted a regulation that, in essence, applied the basic reasoning of the Court of Appeals here, precluding use of the "bubble concept" in nonattainment States' programs designed to enhance air quality. However, when a new administration took office 1981, the EPA, in promulgating the regulations involved here, reevaluated the various arguments that had been advanced in connection with the proper definition of the term "source" and concluded that the term should be given the plantwide definition in nonattainment areas. Pp. 2787–2790.

(e) Parsing the general terms in the text of the amended Clean Air Act—particularly the provisions of §§ 302(j) and 111(a)(3) pertaining to the definition of "source"—does not reveal any actual intent of Congress as to the issue in these cases. To the extent any congressional "intent" can be discerned from the statutory language, it would appear that the listing of overlapping, illustrative terms was intended to enlarge, rather than to confine, the scope of the EPA's power to regulate particular sources in order to effectuate the policies of the Clean Air Act. Similarly, the legislative history is consistent with the ****2780** view that the EPA should have broad discretion in implementing the policies of the 1977 Amendments. The plantwide definition is fully consistent with the policy of allowing reasonable economic growth, and the EPA has advanced a reasonable explanation for its conclusion that the regulations serve environmental objectives as well. The fact that the EPA has from time to time changed its interpretation of the term "source" does not lead to the conclusion that no deference should be accorded the EPA's interpretation of the statute. An agency, to engage in informed rulemaking, must consider varying interpretations and the wisdom of its policy on a continuing basis. Policy arguments concerning the "bubble concept" should be addressed to legislators or administrators, not to judges. The EPA's interpretation of the statute here represents a reasonable accommodation of manifestly competing interests and is entitled to deference. Pp. 2790–2793.

222 U.S.App.D.C. 268, 685 F.2d 718 (1982), reversed.
Deputy Solicitor General Bator argued the cause for petitioners in all cases. With him on the briefs for petitioner in No. 82-1591 were *Solicitor General Lee, Acting Assistant Attorney General Habicht, Deputy Assistant Attorney General Walker, Mark I. Levy, Anne S. Almy, William F. Pedersen,* and *Charles S. Carter. Michael H. Salinsky* and *Kevin M. Fong* filed briefs for petitioner in No. 82-1005. *Robert A. Emmett, David Ferber, Stark Ritchie, Theodore L. Garrett, Patricia A. Barald, Louis E. Tosi, William L. Patberg, Charles F. Lettow,* and *Barton C. Green* filed briefs for petitioners in No. 82-1247.

***839** *David D. Doniger* argued the cause and filed a brief for respondents.†>>>

† Briefs of *amici curiae* urging reversal were filed for the American Gas Association by *John A. Myler;* for the Mid-America Legal Foundation by *John M. Cannon, Susan W. Wanat,* and *Ann P. Sheldon;* and for the Pacific Legal Foundation by *Ronald A. Zumbrun* and *Robin L. Rivett.*

A brief of *amici curiae* urging affirmance was filed for the Commonwealth of Pennsylvania et al. by *LeRoy S. Zimmerman,* Attorney General of Pennsylvania, *Thomas Y. Au, Duane Woodard,* Attorney General of Colorado, *Richard L. Griffith,* Assistant Attorney General, *Joseph I. Lieberman,* Attorney General of Connecticut, *Robert A. Whitehead, Jr.,* Assistant Attorney General, *James S. Tierney,* Attorney General of Maine, *Robert Abrams,* Attorney General of New York, *Marcia J. Cleveland* and *Mary L. Lyndon,* Assistant Attorneys General, *Irwin I. Kimmelman,* Attorney General of New Jersey, *John J. Easton, Jr.,* Attorney General of Vermont, *Merideth Wright,* Assistant Attorney General, *Bronson C. La Follette,* Attorney General of Wisconsin, and *Maryann Sumi,* Assistant Attorney General.

James D. English, Mary-Win O'Brien, and *Bernard Kleiman* filed a brief for the United Steelworkers of America, AFL-CIO-CLC, as *amicus curiae.*

Justice STEVENS delivered the opinion of the Court.

In the Clean Air Act Amendments of 1977, Pub.L. 95–95, 91 Stat. 685, Congress enacted certain requirements applicable***840** to States that had not achieved the national air quality standards established by the

Environmental Protection Agency (EPA) pursuant to earlier legislation. The amended Clean Air Act required these "nonattainment" States to establish a permit program regulating "new or modified major stationary sources" of air pollution. Generally, a permit may not be issued for a new or modified major stationary source unless several stringent conditions are met.[FN1] The EPA regulation promulgated to implement this permit requirement allows a State to adopt a plantwide definition of the term "stationary source." [FN2] Under this definition, an existing plant that contains several pollution-emitting devices may install or modify one piece of equipment without meeting the permit conditions if the alteration will not increase the total emissions from the plant. The question presented by these cases is whether EPA's decision to allow States to treat all of the pollution-emitting devices within the same industrial grouping as though they were encased within a single "bubble" is based on a reasonable construction of the statutory term "stationary source."

FN1. Section 172(b)(6), 42 U.S.C. § 7502(b)(6), provides:

"The plan provisions required by subsection (a) shall—

.....

"(6) require permits for the construction and operation of new or modified major stationary sources in accordance with section 173 (relating to permit requirements)." 91 Stat. 747.

FN2. "(i) 'Stationary source' means any building, structure, facility, or installation which emits or may emit any air pollutant subject to regulation under the Act.

"(ii) 'Building, structure, facility, or installation' means all of the pollutant-emitting activities which belong to the same industrial grouping, are located on one or more contiguous or adjacent properties, and are under the control of the same person (or persons under common control) except the activities of any vessel." 40 CFR §§ 51.18(j)(1)(i) and (ii) (1983).

I

The EPA regulations containing the plantwide definition of the term stationary source were promulgated on October ***841** 14, 1981. 46 Fed.Reg. 50766. Respondents [FN3] filed a timely petition for review in the United States Court of Appeals for the District of Columbia Circuit pursuant to 42 U.S.C. § 7607(b)(1).[FN4] The Court of Appeals ****2781** set aside the regulations. Natural Resources Defense Council, Inc. v. Gorsuch, 222 U.S.App.D.C. 268, 685 F.2d 718 (1982).

FN3. National Resources Defense Council, Inc., Citizens for a Better Environment, Inc., and North Western Ohio Lung Association, Inc.

FN4. Petitioners, Chevron U.S.A. Inc., American Iron and Steel Institute, American Petroleum Institute, Chemical Manufacturers Association, Inc., General Motors Corp., and Rubber Manufacturers Association were granted leave to intervene and argue in support of the regulation.

The court observed that the relevant part of the amended Clean Air Act "does not explicitly define what Congress envisioned as a 'stationary source, to which the permit program ... should apply," and further stated that the precise issue was not "squarely addressed in the legislative history." Id., at 273, 685 F.2d, at 723. In light of its conclusion that the legislative history bearing on the question was "at best contradictory," it reasoned that "the purposes of the nonattainment program should guide our decision here." Id., at 276, n. 39, 685 F.2d, at 726, n. 39.[FN5] Based on two of its precedents concerning the applicability of the bubble concept to certain Clean Air Act programs,[FN6] the court stated that the bubble concept was "mandatory" in programs designed merely to maintain existing air quality, but held that it was "inappropriate" in programs enacted to improve air quality. Id., at 276, 685 F.2d, at 726. Since the purpose of the permit***842** program—its "raison d'être," in the court's view—was to improve air quality, the court held that the bubble concept was inapplicable in these cases under its prior precedents. Ibid. It therefore set aside the regulations embodying the bubble concept as contrary to law. We granted certiorari to review that judgment, 461 U.S. 956, 103 S.Ct. 2427, 77 L.Ed.2d 1314 (1983), and we now reverse.

FN5. The court remarked in this regard:

"We regret, of course, that Congress did not advert specifically to the bubble concept's application to various Clean Air Act programs, and note that a further clarifying statutory directive would facilitate the work of the agency and of the court in their endeavors to serve the legislators' will." 222 U.S.App.D.C., at 276, n. 39, 685 F.2d, at 726, n. 39.

FN6. Alabama Power Co. v. Costle, 204 U.S.App.D.C. 51, 636 F.2d 323 (1979); ASARCO Inc. v. EPA, 188 U.S.App.D.C. 77, 578 F.2d 319 (1978).

[1] The basic legal error of the Court of Appeals was to adopt a static judicial definition of the term "stationary source" when it had decided that Congress itself had not commanded that definition. Respondents do not defend the legal reasoning of the Court of Appeals.FN7 Nevertheless, since this Court reviews judgments, not opinions,FN8 we must determine whether the Court of Appeals' legal error resulted in an erroneous judgment on the validity of the regulations.

FN7. Respondents argued below that EPA's plantwide definition of "stationary source" is contrary to the terms, legislative history, and purposes of the amended Clean Air Act. The court below rejected respondents' arguments based on the language and legislative history of the Act. It did agree with respondents contention that the regulations were inconsistent with the purposes of the Act, but did not adopt the construction of the statute advanced by respondents here. Respondents rely on the arguments rejected by the Court of Appeals in support of the judgment, and may rely on any ground that finds support in the record. See Ryerson v. United States, 312 U.S. 405, 408, 61 S.Ct. 656, 658, 85 L.Ed. 917 (1941); LeTulle v. Scofield, 308 U.S. 415, 421, 60 S.Ct. 313, 316, 84 L.Ed. 355 (1940); Langnes v. Green, 282 U.S. 531, 533–539, 51 S.Ct. 243, 244–246, 75 L.Ed. 520 (1931).

FN8. E.g., Black v. Cutter Laboratories, 351 U.S. 292, 297, 76 S.Ct. 824, 827, 100 L.Ed. 1188 (1956); J.E. Riley Investment Co. v.

Commissioner, 311 U.S. 55, 59, 61 S.Ct. 95, 97, 85 L.Ed. 36 (1940); Williams v. Norris, 12 Wheat. 117, 120, 6 L.Ed. 571 (1827); McClung v. Silliman, 6 Wheat. 598, 603, 5 L.Ed. 340 (1821).

II

[2][3][4] When a court reviews an agency's construction of the statute which it administers, it is confronted with two questions. First, always, is the question whether Congress has directly spoken to the precise question at issue. If the intent of Congress is clear, that is the end of the matter; for the court, ***843** as well as the agency, must give effect to the unambiguously expressed intent of Congress.[FN9] If, however, ****2782** the court determines Congress has not directly addressed the precise question at issue, the court does not simply impose its own construction on the statute, [FN10] as would be necessary in the absence of an administrative interpretation. Rather, if the statute is silent or ambiguous with respect to the specific issue, the question for the court is whether the agency's answer is based on a permissible construction of the statute.[FN11]

FN9. The judiciary is the final authority on issues of statutory construction and must reject administrative constructions which are contrary to clear congressional intent. See, e.g., FEC v. Democratic Senatorial Campaign Committee, 454 U.S. 27, 32, 102 S.Ct. 38, 42, 70 L.Ed.2d 23 (1981); SEC v. Sloan, 436 U.S. 103, 117–118, 98 S.Ct. 1702, 1711–1712, 56 L.Ed.2d 148 (1978); FMC v. Seatrain Lines, Inc., 411 U.S. 726, 745–746, 93 S.Ct. 1773, 1784–1785, 36 L.Ed.2d 620 (1973); Volkswagenwerk v. FMC, 390 U.S. 261, 272, 88 S.Ct. 929, 935, 19 L.Ed.2d 1090 (1968); NLRB v. Brown, 380 U.S. 278, 291, 85 S.Ct. 980, 988, 13 L.Ed.2d 839 (1965); FTC v. Colgate–Palmolive Co., 380 U.S. 374, 385, 85 S.Ct. 1035, 1042, 13 L.Ed.2d 904 (1965); Social Security Board v. Nierotko, 327 U.S. 358, 369, 66 S.Ct. 637, 643, 90 L.Ed. 718 (1946); Burnet v. Chicago Portrait Co., 285 U.S. 1, 16, 52 S.Ct. 275, 281, 76 L.Ed. 587 (1932); Webster v. Luther, 163 U.S. 331, 342, 16 S.Ct. 963, 967, 41 L.Ed. 179 (1896). If a court, employing traditional tools of statutory construction, ascertains that Congress had an intention on the precise question at issue, that intention is the law and must be given effect.

FN10. See generally, R. Pound, The Spirit of the Common Law 174–175 (1921).

FN11. The court need not conclude that the agency construction was the only one it permissibly could have adopted to uphold the construction, or even the reading the court would have reached if the question initially had arisen in a judicial proceeding. FEC v. Democratic Senatorial Campaign Committee, 454 U.S., at 39, 102 S.Ct., at 46; Zenith Radio Corp. v. United States, 437 U.S. 443, 450, 98 S.Ct. 2441, 2445, 57 L.Ed.2d 337 (1978); Train v. Natural Resources Defense Council, Inc., 421 U.S. 60, 75, 95 S.Ct. 1470, 1479, 43 L.Ed.2d 731 (1975); Udall v. Tallman, 380 U.S. 1, 16, 85 S.Ct. 792, 801, 13 L.Ed.2d 616 (1965); Unemployment Compensation Comm'n v. Aragon, 329 U.S. 143, 153, 67 S.Ct. 245, 250, 91 L.Ed. 136 (1946); McLaren v. Fleischer, 256 U.S. 477, 480–481, 41 S.Ct. 577, 577–578, 65 L.Ed. 1052 (1921).

[5] "The power of an administrative agency to administer a congressionally created ... program necessarily requires the formulation of policy and the making of rules to fill any gap left, implicitly or explicitly, by Congress." Morton v. Ruiz, 415 U.S. 199, 231, 94 S.Ct. 1055, 1072, 39 L.Ed.2d 270 (1974). If Congress has explicitly left a gap for the agency to fill, there is an express delegation ***844** of authority to the agency to elucidate a specific provision of the statute by regulation. Such legislative regulations are given controlling weight unless they are arbitrary, capricious, or manifestly contrary to the statute.[FN12] Sometimes the legislative delegation to an agency on a particular question is implicit rather than explicit. In such a case, a court may not substitute its own construction of a statutory provision for a reasonable interpretation made by the administrator of an agency.[FN13]

FN12. See, e.g., United States v. Morton, 467 U.S. 822, 834, 104 S.Ct. 2769, 2776, 81 L.Ed.2d 680 (1984) Schweiker v. Gray Panthers, 453 U.S. 34, 44, 101 S.Ct. 2633, 2640, 69 L.Ed.2d 460 (1981); Batterton v. Francis, 432 U.S. 416, 424–426, 97 S.Ct. 2399, 2404–2406, 53 L.Ed.2d 448 (1977); American Telephone & Telegraph Co. v. United States, 299 U.S. 232, 235–237, 57 S.Ct. 170, 172–173, 81 L.Ed. 142 (1936).

FN13. E.g., INS v. Jong Ha Wang, 450 U.S. 139, 144, 101 S.Ct. 1027, 1031, 67 L.Ed.2d 123 (1981); Train v. Natural Resources Defense Council, Inc., 421 U.S., at 87, 95 S.Ct., at 1485.

[6] We have long recognized that considerable weight should be accorded to an executive department's construction of a statutory scheme it is entrusted to administer,FN14 and the principle of deference to administrative interpretations.

FN14. Aluminum Co. of America v. Central Lincoln Peoples' Util. Dist., 467 U.S. 380, 389, 104 S.Ct. 2472, 2479–2480, 81 L.Ed.2d 301 (1984); Blum v. Bacon, 457 U.S. 132, 141, 102 S.Ct. 2355, 2361, 72 L.Ed.2d 728 (1982); Union Electric Co. v. EPA, 427 U.S. 246, 256, 96 S.Ct. 2518, 2525, 49 L.Ed.2d 474 (1976); Investment Company Institute v. Camp, 401 U.S. 617, 626–627, 91 S.Ct. 1091, 1097, 28 L.Ed.2d 367 (1971); Unemployment Compensation Comm'n v. Aragon, 329 U.S., at 153–154, 67 S.Ct., at 250–251; NLRB v. Hearst Publications, Inc., 322 U.S. 111, 131, 64 S.Ct. 851, 860, 88 L.Ed. 1170 (1944); McLaren v. Fleischer, 256 U.S., at 480–481, 41 S.Ct., at 577–578; Webster v. Luther, 163 U.S., at 342, 16 S.Ct., at 967; Brown v. United States, 113 U.S. 568, 570–571, 5 S.Ct. 648, 649–650, 28 L.Ed. 1079 (1885); United States v. Moore, 95 U.S. 760, 763, 24 L.Ed. 588 (1878); Edwards' Lessee v. Darby, 12 Wheat. 206, 210, 6 L.Ed. 603 (1827).

"has been consistently followed by this Court whenever decision as to the meaning or reach of a statute has involved reconciling conflicting policies, and a full ****2783** understanding of the force of the statutory policy in the given situation has depended upon more than ordinary knowledge respecting the matters subjected to agency regulations. See, e.g., National Broadcasting Co. v. United States, 319 U.S. 190 [63 S.Ct. 997, 87 L.Ed. 1344]; Labor Board v. Hearst Publications, Inc., 322 U.S. 111 [64 S.Ct. 851, 88 L.Ed. 1170]; ***845**Republic Aviation Corp. v. Labor Board, 324 U.S. 793 [65 S.Ct. 982, 89 L.Ed. 1372]; Securities & Exchange Comm'n v. Chenery Corp., [332] 322 U.S. 194 [67 S.Ct. 1575, 91 L.Ed. 1995]; Labor Board v. Seven–Up Bottling Co., 344 U.S. 344 [73 S.Ct. 287, 97 L.Ed. 377].

"... If this choice represents a reasonable accommodation of conflicting policies that were committed to the agency's care by the statute, we should not disturb it unless it appears from the statute or its legislative history that the accommodation is not one that Congress would have sanctioned." United States v. Shimer, 367 U.S. 374, 382, 383, 81 S.Ct. 1554, 1560, 1561, 6 L.Ed.2d 908 (1961).

Accord Capital Cities Cable, Inc. v. Crisp, 467 U.S. 691, 699–700, 104 S.Ct. 2694, 2700–2701, 81 L.Ed.2d 580 (1984).

In light of these well-settled principles it is clear that the Court of Appeals misconceived the nature of its role in reviewing the regulations at issue. Once it determined, after its own examination of the legislation, that Congress did not actually have an intent regarding the applicability of the bubble concept to the permit program, the question before it was not whether in its view the concept is "inappropriate" in the general context of a program designed to improve air quality, but whether the Administrator's view that it is appropriate in the context of this particular program is a reasonable one. Based on the examination of the legislation and its history which follows, we agree with the Court of Appeals that Congress did not have a specific intention on the applicability of the bubble concept in these cases, and conclude that the EPA's use of that concept here is a reasonable policy choice for the agency to make.

III

In the 1950's and the 1960's Congress enacted a series of statutes designed to encourage and to assist the States in curtailing air pollution. See generally Train v. Natural Resources Defense Council, Inc., 421 U.S. 60, 63–64, 95 S.Ct. 1470, 1474–1475, 43 L.Ed.2d 731 (1975). The Clean Air Amendments of 1970, Pub.L. 91–604, 84 Stat. 1676, "sharply increased federal authority and responsibility ***846** in the continuing effort to combat air pollution," 421 U.S., at 64, 95 S.Ct., at 1474, but continued to assign "primary responsibility for assuring air quality" to the several States, 84 Stat. 1678. Section 109 of the 1970 Amendments directed the EPA to promulgate National Ambient Air Quality Standards (NAAQS's) FN15 and § 110 directed the States to develop plans (SIP's) to implement the standards within specified deadlines. In addition, § 111 provided that major new sources of pollution would be required to conform to technology-based performance standards; the EPA was directed to publish a list of categories of sources of pollution and to establish new source performance standards (NSPS) for each. Section 111(e) prohibited the operation of any new source in violation of a performance standard.

FN15. Primary standards were defined as those whose attainment and maintenance were necessary to protect the public health, and secondary standards were intended to specify a level of air quality that would protect the public welfare.

Section 111(a) defined the terms that are to be used in setting and enforcing standards of performance for new stationary sources. It provided:

"For purposes of this section:

.....

"(3) The term 'stationary source' means any building, structure, facility, or installation which emits or may emit any air pollutant." 84 Stat. 1683.

****2784** In the 1970 Amendments that definition was not only applicable to the NSPS program required by § 111, but also was made applicable to a requirement of § 110 that each state implementation plan contain a procedure for reviewing the location of any proposed new source and preventing its construction if it would preclude the attainment or maintenance of national air quality standards. FN16

FN16. See §§ 110(a)(2)(D) and 110(a)(4).

In due course, the EPA promulgated NAAQS's, approved SIP's, and adopted detailed regulations governing NSPS's ***847** for various categories of equipment. In one of its programs, the EPA used a plantwide definition of the term "stationary source." In 1974, it issued NSPS's for the nonferrous smelting industry that provided that the standards would not apply to the modification of major smelting units if their increased emissions were offset by reductions in other portions of the same plant.FN17

FN17. The Court of Appeals ultimately held that this plantwide approach was prohibited by the 1970 Act, see ASARCO Inc., 188 U.S.App.D.C., at 83–84, 578 F.2d, at 325–327. This decision was rendered after enactment of the 1977 Amendments, and hence the standard was in effect when Congress enacted the 1977 Amendments.

Nonattainment

The 1970 legislation provided for the attainment of primary NAAQS's by 1975. In many areas of the country, particularly the most industrialized States, the statutory goals were not attained.FN18 In 1976, the 94th Congress was confronted with this fundamental problem, as well as many others respecting pollution control. As always in this area, the legislative struggle was basically between interests seeking strict schemes to reduce pollution rapidly to eliminate its social costs and interests advancing the economic concern that strict schemes would retard industrial development with attendant social costs. The 94th Congress, confronting these competing interests, was unable to agree on what response was in the public interest: legislative proposals to deal with nonattainment failed to command the necessary consensus.FN19

FN18. See Report of the National Commission on Air Quality, To Breathe Clean Air, 3.3–20 through 3.3–33 (1981).

FN19. Comprehensive bills did pass both Chambers of Congress; the Conference Report was rejected in the Senate. 122 Cong.Rec. 34375–34403, 34405–34418 (1976).

In light of this situation, the EPA published an Emissions Offset Interpretative Ruling in December 1976, see 41 Fed.Reg. 55524, to "fill the gap," as respondents put it, until Congress acted. The Ruling stated that it was intended to ***848** address "the issue of whether and to what extent national air quality standards established under the Clean Air Act may restrict or prohibit growth of major new or expanded stationary air pollution sources." Id., at 55524–55525. In general, the Ruling provided that "a major new source may locate in an area with air quality worse than a national standard only if stringent conditions can be met." Id., at 55525. The Ruling gave primary emphasis to the rapid attainment of the statute's environmental goals. FN20 Consistent with that emphasis, the construction of every new source in nonattainment areas had to meet the "lowest achievable emission rate" under the current state of the art for that type of facility. See Ibid. The 1976 Ruling did not, however, explicitly adopt or reject the "bubble concept." FN21

FN20. For example, it stated:

"Particularly with regard to the primary NAAQS's, Congress and the Courts have made clear that economic considerations must be subordinated to NAAQS achievement and maintenance. While the ruling allows for some growth in areas violating a NAAQS if the net effect is to insure further progress toward NAAQS achievement, the Act does not allow economic growth to be accommodated at the expense of the public health." 41 Fed.Reg. 55527 (1976).

FN21. In January 1979, the EPA noted that the 1976 Ruling was ambiguous concerning this issue:

"A number of commenters indicated the need for a more explicit definition of 'source.' Some readers found that it was unclear under the 1976 Ruling whether a plant with a number of different processes and emission points would be considered a single source. The changes set forth below define a source as 'any structure, building, facility, equipment, installation, or operation (or combination thereof) which is located on one or more contiguous or adjacent properties and which is owned or operated by the same person (or by persons under common control.' This definition precludes a large plant from being separated into individual production lines for purposes of determining applicability of the offset requirements." 44 Fed.Reg. 3276.

****2785** IV

The Clean Air Act Amendments of 1977 are a lengthy, detailed, technical, complex, and comprehensive response to a major social issue. A small portion of the statute—91 Stat. ***849** 745–751 (Part D of Title I of the amended Act, 42 U.S.C. §§ 7501–7508)—expressly deals with nonattainment areas. The focal point of this controversy is one phrase in that portion of the Amendments.FN22

FN22. Specifically, the controversy in these cases involves the meaning of the term "major stationary sources" in § 172(b)(6) of the Act, 42 U.S.C. § 7502(b)(6). The meaning of the term "proposed source" in § 173(2) of the Act, 42 U.S.C. § 7503(2), is not at issue.

Basically, the statute required each State in a nonattainment area to prepare and obtain approval of a new SIP by July 1, 1979. In the interim those States were required to comply with the EPA's interpretative Ruling of December 21, 1976. 91 Stat. 745. The deadline for attainment of the primary NAAQS's was extended until December 31, 1982, and in some cases until December 31, 1987, but the SIP's were required to contain a number of provisions designed to achieve the goals as expeditiously as possible.FN23

FN23. Thus, among other requirements, § 172(b) provided that the SIP's shall—

"(3) require, in the interim, reasonable further progress (as defined in section 171(1)) including such reduction in emissions from existing sources in the area as may be obtained through the adoption, at a minimum, of reasonably available control technology;

"(4) include a comprehensive, accurate, current inventory of actual emissions from all sources (as provided by rule of the Administrator) of each such pollutant for each such area which is revised and resubmitted as frequently as may be necessary to assure that the requirements of paragraph (3) are met and to assess the need for additional reductions to assure attainment of each standard by the date required under paragraph (1);

"(5) expressly identify and quantify the emissions, if any, of any such pollutant which will be allowed to result from the construction and operation of major new or modified stationary sources for each such area; ...

.....

"(8) contain emission limitations, schedules of compliance and such other measures as may be necessary to meet the requirements of this section." 91 Stat. 747.

Section 171(1) provided:

"(1) The term 'reasonable further progress' means annual incremental reductions in emissions of the applicable air pollutant (including substantial reductions in the early years following approval or promulgation of plan provisions under this part and section 110(a)(2)(I) and regular reductions thereafter) which are sufficient in the judgment of the Administrator, to provide for attainment of the applicable national ambient air quality standard by the date required in section 172(a)." Id., at 746.

***850** Most significantly for our purposes, the statute provided that each plan shall

"(6) require permits for the construction and operation of new or modified major stationary sources in accordance with section 173...." Id., 747.

Before issuing a permit, § 173 requires (1) the state agency to determine that there will be sufficient emissions reductions in the region to offset the emissions from the new source and also to allow for reasonable further progress toward attainment, or that the increased emissions will not exceed an allowance for growth established pursuant to § 172(b)(5); (2) the applicant to certify that his other sources in the State are in compliance with the SIP, (3) the agency to determine that the applicable SIP is otherwise being implemented, and (4) the proposed source to comply with the lowest achievable emission rate (LAER).FN24

FN24. Section 171(3) provides:

"(3) The term 'lowest achievable emission rate' means for any source, that rate of emissions which reflects—

"(A) the most stringent emission limitation which is contained in the implementation plan of any State for such class or category of source, unless the owner or operator of the proposed source demonstrates that such limitations are not achievable, or

"(B) the most stringent emission limitation which is achieved in practice by such class or category of source, whichever is more stringent. "In no event shall the application of this term permit a proposed new or modified source to emit any pollutant in excess of the amount allowable under applicable new source standards of performance."

The LAER requirement is defined in terms that make it even more stringent than the applicable new source performance standard developed under § 111 of the Act, as amended by the 1970 statute.

****2786 *851** The 1977 Amendments contain no specific reference to the "bubble concept." Nor do they contain a specific definition of the term "stationary source," though they did not disturb the definition of "stationary source" contained in § 111(a)(3), applicable by the terms of the Act to the NSPS program. Section 302(j), however, defines the term "major stationary source" as follows:

"(j) Except as otherwise expressly provided, the terms 'major stationary source' and 'major emitting facility' mean any stationary facility or source of air pollutants which directly emits, or has the potential to emit, one hundred tons per year or more of any air pollutant (including any major emitting facility or source of fugitive emissions of any such pollutant, as determined by rule by the Administrator)." 91 Stat. 770.

V

The legislative history of the portion of the 1977 Amendments dealing with nonattainment areas does not contain any specific comment on the "bubble concept" or the question whether a plantwide definition of a stationary source is permissible under the permit program. It does, however, plainly disclose that in the permit program Congress sought to accommodate the conflict between the economic interest in permitting capital improvements to continue and the environmental interest in improving air quality. Indeed, the

House Committee Report identified the economic interest as one of the "two main purposes" of this section of the bill. It stated:

"Section 117 of the bill, adopted during full committee markup establishes a new section 127 of the Clean Air Act. The section has two main purposes: (1) to allow reasonable economic growth to continue in an area while making reasonable further progress to assure attainment of the standards by a fixed date; and (2) to allow ***852** States greater flexibility for the former purpose than EPA's present interpretative regulations afford.

"The new provision allows States with nonattainment areas to pursue one of two options. First, the State may proceed under EPA's present 'tradeoff' or 'offset' ruling. The Administrator is authorized, moreover, to modify or amend that ruling in accordance with the intent and purposes of this section.

"The State's second option would be to revise its implementation plan in accordance with this new provision." H.R.Rep. No. 95–294, p. 211 (1977), U.S.Code Cong. & Admin.News 1977, pp. 1077, 1290.[FN25]

FN25. During the floor debates Congressman Waxman remarked that the legislation struck

"a proper balance between environmental controls and economic growth in the dirty air areas of America.... There is no other single issue which more clearly poses the conflict between pollution control and new jobs. We have determined that neither need be compromised....

"This is a fair and balanced approach, which will not undermine our economic vitality, or impede achievement of our ultimate environmental objectives." 123 Cong.Rec. 27076 (1977).

The second "main purpose" of the provision—allowing the States "greater flexibility" than the EPA's interpretative Ruling—as well as the reference to the EPA's authority to amend its Ruling in accordance with the intent of the section, is entirely consistent with the view that Congress did not intend to freeze the definition of "source" contained in the existing regulation into a rigid statutory requirement.

The portion of the Senate Committee Report dealing with nonattainment areas states generally that it was intended to "supersede the EPA administrative approach," and that expansion should be permitted if a State could "demonstrate that these facilities can be accommodated within its overall plan to provide for attainment of air quality standards." S.Rep. No. 95–127, ****2787** p. 55 (1977). The Senate Report notes the value of "case-by-case review of each new or modified major source of pollution that seeks to locate in a region exceeding an ambient standard," explaining that such a review "requires matching reductions from existing sources against ***853** emissions expected from the new source in order to assure that introduction of the new source will not prevent attainment of the applicable standard by the statutory deadline." Ibid. This description of a case-by-case approach to plant additions, which emphasizes the net consequences of the construction or modification of a new source, as well as its impact on the overall achievement of the national standards, was not, however, addressed to the precise issue raised by these cases.

Senator Muskie made the following remarks:

"I should note that the test for determining whether a new or modified source is subject to the EPA interpretative regulation [the Offset Ruling]—and to the permit requirements of the revised implementation plans under the conference bill—is whether the source will emit a pollutant into an area which is exceeding a national ambient air quality standard for that pollutant—or precursor. Thus, a new source is still subject to such requirements as 'lowest achievable emission rate' even if it is constructed as a replacement for an older facility resulting in a net reduction from previous emission levels.

"A source—including an existing facility ordered to convert to coal—is subject to all the nonattainment requirements as a modified source if it makes any physical change which increases the amount of any air pollutant for which the standards in the area are exceeded." 123 Cong.Rec. 26847 (1977).

VI

As previously noted, prior to the 1977 Amendments, the EPA had adhered to a plantwide definition of the term "source" under a NSPS program. After adoption of the 1977 Amendments, proposals for a plantwide definition were considered in at least three formal proceedings.

In January 1979, the EPA considered the question whether the same restriction on new construction in nonattainment areas that had been included in its December 1976 Ruling ***854** should be required in the revised SIP's that were scheduled to go into effect in July 1979. After noting that the 1976 Ruling was ambiguous on the question "whether a plant with a number of different processes and emission points would be considered a single source," 44 Fed.Reg. 3276 (1979), the EPA, in effect, provided a bifurcated answer to that question. In those areas that did not have a revised SIP in effect by July 1979, the EPA rejected the plantwide definition; on the other hand, it expressly concluded that the plantwide approach would be permissible in certain circumstances if authorized by an approved SIP. It stated:

"Where a state implementation plan is revised and implemented to satisfy the requirements of Part D, including the reasonable further progress requirement, the plan requirements for major modifications may exempt modifications of existing facilities that are accompanied by intrasource offsets so that there is no net increase in emissions. The agency endorses such exemptions, which would provide greater flexibility to sources to effectively manage their air emissions at least cost." Ibid.[FN26]

FN26. In the same Ruling, the EPA added:

"The above exemption is permitted under the SIP because, to be approved under Part D, plan revisions due by January 1979 must contain adopted measures assuring that reasonable further progress will be made. Furthermore, in most circumstances, the measures adopted by January 1979 must be sufficient to actually provide for attainment of the standards by the dates required under the Act, and in all circumstances measures adopted by 1982 must provide for attainment. See Section 172 of the Act and 43 FR 21673–21677 (May 19, 1978). Also, Congress intended under Section 173 of the Act that States would have some latitude to depart from the strict requirements of this Ruling when the State plan is revised and is being carried out in accordance with Part D. Under a Part D plan, therefore, there is less need to subject a modification of an existing facility to LAER and other stringent requirements if the modification is accompanied by sufficient intrasource offsets so that there is no net increase in emissions." 44 Fed.Reg. 3277 (1979).

****2788 *855** In April, and again in September 1979, the EPA published additional comments in which it indicated that revised SIP's could adopt the plantwide definition of source in nonattainment areas in certain circumstances. See id., at 20372, 20379, 51924, 51951, 51958. On the latter occasion, the EPA made a formal rulemaking proposal that would have permitted the use of the "bubble concept" for new installations within a plant as well as for modifications of existing units. It explained:

" 'Bubble' Exemption: The use of offsets inside the same source is called the 'bubble.' EPA proposes use of the definition of 'source' (see above) to limit the use of the bubble under nonattainment requirements in the following respects:

"i. Part D SIPs that include all requirements needed to assure reasonable further progress and attainment by the deadline under section 172 and that are being carried out need not restrict the use of a plantwide bubble, the same as under the PSD proposal.

"ii. Part D SIPs that do not meet the requirements specified must limit use of the bubble by including a definition of 'installation' as an identifiable piece of process equipment." FN27

FN27. Id., at 51926. Later in that Ruling, the EPA added:

"However, EPA believes that complete Part D SIPs, which contain adopted and enforceable requirements sufficient to assure attainment, may apply the approach proposed above for PSD, with plant-wide review but no review of individual pieces of equipment. Use of only a plant-wide definition of source will permit plant-wide offsets for avoiding NSR of new or modified pieces of equipment. However, this is only appropriate once a SIP is adopted that will assure the reductions in existing emissions necessary for attainment. See 44 FR 3276 col. 3 (January 16, 1979). If the level of emissions allowed in the SIP is low enough to assure reasonable further progress and attainment, new construction or modifications with enough offset credit to prevent an emission increase should not jeopardize attainment." Id., at 51933.

***856** Significantly, the EPA expressly noted that the word "source" might be given a plantwide definition for some purposes and a narrower definition for other purposes. It wrote:

"Source means any building structure, facility, or installation which emits or may emit any regulated pollutant. 'Building, structure, facility or installation' means plant in PSD areas and in nonattainment areas except where the growth prohibitions would apply or where no adequate SIP exists or is being carried out." Id., at 51925.[FN28]

FN28. In its explanation of why the use of the "bubble concept" was especially appropriate in preventing significant deterioration (PSD) in clean air areas, the EPA stated: "In addition, application of the bubble on a plant-wide basis encourages voluntary upgrading of equipment, and growth in productive capacity." Id., at 51932.

The EPA's summary of its proposed Ruling discloses a flexible rather than rigid definition of the term "source" to implement various policies and programs:

"In summary, EPA is proposing two different ways to define source for different kinds of NSR programs:

"(1) For PSD and complete Part D SIPs, review would apply only to plants, with an unrestricted plant-wide bubble.

"(2) For the offset ruling, restrictions on construction, and incomplete Part D SIPs, review would apply to both plants and individual pieces of process equipment, causing the plant-wide bubble not to apply for new and modified major pieces of equipment.

"In addition, for the restrictions on construction, EPA is proposing to define 'major modification' so as to prohibit the bubble entirely. Finally, an alternative discussed but not favored is to have only pieces of process equipment reviewed, resulting in no plant-wide bubble and allowing minor pieces of equipment to escape**2789 NSR *857 regardless of whether they are within a major plant." Id., at 51934.

In August 1980, however, the EPA adopted a regulation that, in essence, applied the basic reasoning of the Court of Appeals in these cases. The EPA took particular note of the two then-recent Court of Appeals decisions, which had created the bright-line rule that the "bubble concept" should be employed in a program designed to maintain air quality but not in one designed to enhance air quality. Relying heavily on those cases,[FN29] EPA adopted a dual definition of "source" for nonattainment areas that required a permit whenever a change in either the entire plant, or one of its components, would result in a significant increase in emissions even if the increase was completely offset by reductions elsewhere in the plant. The EPA expressed the opinion that this interpretation was "more consistent with congressional intent" than the plantwide definition because it "would bring in more sources or modifications for review," 45 Fed.Reg. 52697 (1980), but its primary legal analysis was predicated on the two Court of Appeals decisions.

FN29. "The dual definition also is consistent with Alabama Power and ASARCO. Alabama Power held that EPA had broad discretion to define the constituent terms of 'source' so as best to effectuate the purposes of the statute. Different definitions of 'source' can therefore be used for different sections of the statute....

"Moreover, Alabama Power and ASARCO taken together suggest that there is a distinction between Clean Air Act programs designed to enhance air quality and those designed only to maintain air quality....

.....

"Promulgation of the dual definition follows the mandate of Alabama Power, which held that, while EPA could not define 'source' as a combination of sources, EPA had broad discretion to define 'building,' 'structure,' 'facility,' and 'installation' so as to best accomplish the purposes of the Act." 45 Fed.Reg. 52697 (1980).

In 1981 a new administration took office and initiated a "Government-wide reexamination of regulatory burdens and complexities." 46 Fed.Reg. 16281. In the context of that ***858** review, the EPA reevaluated the various arguments that had been advanced in connection with the proper definition of the term "source" and concluded that the term should be given the same definition in both nonattainment areas and PSD areas.

In explaining its conclusion, the EPA first noted that the definitional issue was not squarely addressed in either the statute or its legislative history and therefore that the issue involved an agency "judgment as how to best carry out the Act." Ibid. It then set forth several reasons for concluding that the plantwide definition was more appropriate. It pointed out that the dual definition "can act as a disincentive to new investment and modernization by discouraging modifications to existing facilities" and "can actually retard progress in air pollution control by discouraging replacement of older, dirtier processes or pieces of equipment with new, cleaner ones." Ibid. Moreover, the new definition "would simplify EPA's rules by using the same definition of 'source' for PSD, nonattainment new source review and the construction moratorium. This reduces confusion and inconsistency." Ibid. Finally, the agency explained that additional requirements that remained in place would accomplish the fundamental purposes of achieving attainment with NAAQS's as expeditiously as possible.[FN30] These conclusions were ****2790** expressed***859** in a proposed rulemaking in August 1981 that was formally promulgated in October. See id., at 50766.

FN30. It stated:

"5. States will remain subject to the requirement that for all nonattainment areas they demonstrate attainment of NAAQS as expeditiously as practicable and show reasonable further progress toward such attainment. Thus, the proposed change in the mandatory scope of nonattainment new source review should not interfere with the fundamental purpose of Part D of the Act.

"6. New Source Performance Standards (NSPS) will continue to apply to many new or modified facilities and will assure use of the most up-to-date pollution control techniques regardless of the applicability of nonattainment area new source review.

"7. In order to avoid nonattainment area new source review, a major plant undergoing modification must show that it will not experience a significant net increase in emissions. Where overall emissions increase significantly, review will continue to be required." 46 Fed.Reg. 16281 (1981).

VII

[7] In this Court respondents expressly reject the basic rationale of the Court of Appeals' decision. That court viewed the statutory definition of the term "source" as sufficiently flexible to cover either a plantwide definition, a narrower definition covering each unit within a plant, or a dual definition that could apply to both the entire "bubble" and its components. It interpreted the policies of the statute, however, to mandate the plantwide definition in programs designed to maintain clean air and to forbid it in programs designed to improve air quality. Respondents place a fundamentally different construction on the statute. They contend that the text of the Act requires the EPA to use a dual definition—if either a component of a plant, or the plant as a whole, emits over 100 tons of pollutant, it is a major stationary source. They thus contend that the EPA rules adopted in 1980, insofar as they apply to the maintenance of the quality of clean air, as well as the 1981 rules which apply to nonattainment areas, violate the statute.[FN31]

FN31. "What EPA may not do, however, is define all four terms to mean only plants. In the 1980 PSD rules, EPA did just that. EPA compounded the mistake in the 1981 rules here under review, in which it abandoned the dual definition." Brief for Respondents 29, n. 56.

Statutory Language

The definition of the term "stationary source" in § 111(a)(3) refers to "any building, structure, facility, or installation" which emits air pollution. See supra, at 2784. This definition is applicable only to the NSPS program by the express terms of the statute; the text of the statute does not make this definition***860** applicable to the permit program. Petitioners therefore maintain that there is no statutory language even relevant to ascertaining the meaning of stationary source in the permit program aside from § 302(j), which defines the term "major stationary source." See supra, at 2786. We disagree with petitioners on this point.

The definition in § 302(j) tells us what the word "major" means—a source must emit at least 100 tons of pollution to qualify—but it sheds virtually no light on the meaning of the term "stationary source." It does equate a source with a facility—a "major emitting facility" and a "major stationary source" are synonymous under § 302(j). The ordinary meaning of the term "facility" is some collection of integrated elements which has been designed and constructed to achieve some purpose. Moreover, it is certainly no affront to common English usage to take a reference to a major facility or a major source to connote an entire plant as opposed to its constituent parts. Basically, however, the language of § 302(j) simply does not compel any given interpretation of the term "source."

Respondents recognize that, and hence point to § 111(a)(3). Although the definition in that section is not literally applicable to the permit program, it sheds as much light on the meaning of the word "source" as anything in the statute.FN32 As respondents point out, use of the words "building, structure, facility, or installation," as the definition of source, could be read to impose the permit conditions on an individual building that is a part of a plant.FN33 A "word may have a character of its own not to be submerged by its association." ***861**Russell Motor Car Co. v. United States, 261 U.S. 514, 519, 43 S.Ct. 428, 429, 67 L.Ed. 778 (1923). On the other hand, the meaning of a word must be ascertained in the context of achieving particular objectives, and the words associated with it may ****2791** indicate that the true meaning of the series is to convey a common idea. The language may reasonably be interpreted to impose the requirement on any discrete, but integrated, operation which pollutes. This gives meaning to all of the terms—a single building, not part of a larger operation, would be covered if it emits more than 100 tons of pollution, as would any facility, structure, or installation. Indeed, the language itself implies a "bubble concept" of sorts: each enumerated item would seem to be treated as if it were encased in a bubble. While respondents insist that each of these terms must be given a discrete meaning, they also argue that § 111(a)(3) defines "source" as that term is used in § 302(j). The latter section, however, equates a source with a facility, whereas the former defines "source" as a facility, among other items.

FN32. We note that the EPA in fact adopted the language of that definition in its regulations under the permit program. 40 CFR §§ 51.18(j)(1)(i), (ii) (1983).

FN33. Since the regulations give the States the option to define an individual unit as a source, see 40 CFR § 51.18(j)(1) (1983), petitioners do not dispute that the terms can be read as respondents suggest.

We are not persuaded that parsing of general terms in the text of the statute will reveal an actual intent of Congress.[FN34] ***862** We know full well that this language is not dispositive; the terms are overlapping and the language is not precisely directed to the question of the applicability of a given term in the context of a larger operation. To the extent any congressional "intent" can be discerned from this language, it would appear that the listing of overlapping, illustrative terms was intended to enlarge, rather than to confine, the scope of the agency's power to regulate particular sources in order to effectuate the policies of the Act.

FN34. The argument based on the text of § 173, which defines the permit requirements for nonattainment areas, is a classic example of circular reasoning. One of the permit requirements is that "the proposed source is required to comply with the lowest achievable emission rate" (LAER). Although a State may submit a revised SIP that provides for the waiver of another requirement—the "offset condition"—the SIP may not provide for a waiver of the LAER condition for any proposed source. Respondents argue that the plantwide definition of the term "source" makes it unnecessary for newly constructed units within the plant to satisfy the LAER requirement if their emissions are offset by the reductions achieved by the retirement of older equipment. Thus, according to respondents, the plantwide definition allows what the statute explicitly prohibits—the waiver of the LAER requirement for the newly constructed units. But this argument proves nothing because the statute does not prohibit the waiver unless the proposed new unit is indeed subject to the permit program. If it is not, the statute does not impose the LAER requirement at all and there is no need to reach any waiver question. In other words, § 173 of the statute merely deals with the consequences of the definition of the term "source" and does not define the term.

Legislative History

In addition, respondents argue that the legislative history and policies of the Act foreclose the plantwide definition, and that the EPA's interpretation is not entitled to deference because it represents a sharp break with prior interpretations of the Act.

Based on our examination of the legislative history, we agree with the Court of Appeals that it is unilluminating. The general remarks pointed to by respondents "were obviously not made with this narrow issue in mind and they cannot be said to demonstrate a Congressional desire...." Jewell Ridge Coal Corp. v. Mine Workers, 325 U.S. 161, 168–169, 65 S.Ct. 1063, 1067–1068, 89 L.Ed. 1534 (1945). Respondents' argument based on the legislative history relies heavily on Senator Muskie's observation that a new source is subject to the LAER requirement.[FN35] But the full statement is ambiguous and like the text of § 173 itself, this comment does not tell us what a new source is, much less that it is to have an inflexible definition. We find that the legislative history as a whole is silent on the precise issue before us. It is, however, consistent with the view that the EPA should have broad discretion in implementing the policies of the 1977 Amendments.

FN35. See supra, at 2787. We note that Senator Muskie was not critical of the EPA's use of the "bubble concept" in one NSPS program prior to the 1977 amendments. See ibid.

863** More importantly, that history plainly identifies the policy concerns that motivated the enactment; the plantwide definition is fully consistent with one of those concerns*2792** —the allowance of reasonable economic growth—and, whether or not we believe it most effectively implements the other, we must recognize that the EPA has advanced a reasonable explanation for its conclusion that the regulations serve the environmental objectives as well. See supra, at 2789–2790, and n. 29; see also supra, at 2788, n. 27. Indeed, its reasoning is supported by the public record developed in the rulemaking process,[FN36] as well as by certain private studies.[FN37]

FN36. See, for example, the statement of the New York State Department of Environmental Conservation, pointing out that denying a source owner flexibility in selecting options made it "simpler and cheaper to operate old, more polluting sources than to trade up...." App. 128–129.

FN37. "Economists have proposed that economic incentives be substituted for the cumbersome administrative-legal framework. The objective is to make the profit and cost incentives that work so well in the marketplace work for pollution control.... [The 'bubble' or 'netting' concept] is a first attempt in this direction. By giving a plant manager flexibility to find the places and processes within a plant that control emissions most cheaply, pollution control can be achieved more quickly and cheaply." L. Lave & G. Omenn, Cleaning Air: Reforming the Clean Air Act 28 (1981) (footnote omitted).

Our review of the EPA's varying interpretations of the word "source"—both before and after the 1977 Amendments—convinces us that the agency primarily responsible for administering this important legislation has consistently interpreted it flexibly—not in a sterile textual vacuum, but in the context of implementing policy decisions in a technical and complex arena. The fact that the agency has from time to time changed its interpretation of the term "source" does not, as respondents argue, lead us to conclude that no deference should be accorded the agency's interpretation of the statute. An initial agency interpretation is not instantly carved in stone. On the contrary, the agency, to engage in informed rulemaking, must consider varying interpretations ***864** and the wisdom of its policy on a continuing basis. Moreover, the fact that the agency has adopted different definitions in different contexts adds force to the argument that the definition itself is flexible, particularly since Congress has never indicated any disapproval of a flexible reading of the statute.

Significantly, it was not the agency in 1980, but rather the Court of Appeals that read the statute inflexibly to command a plantwide definition for programs designed to maintain clean air and to forbid such a definition for programs designed to improve air quality. The distinction the court drew may well be a sensible one, but our labored review of the problem has surely disclosed that it is not a distinction that Congress ever articulated itself, or one that the EPA found in the statute before the courts began to review the legislative work product. We conclude that it was the Court of Appeals, rather than Congress or any of the decisionmakers who are authorized by Congress to administer this legislation, that was primarily responsible for the 1980 position taken by the agency.

Policy

The arguments over policy that are advanced in the parties' briefs create the impression that respondents are now waging in a judicial forum a specific policy battle which they ultimately lost in the agency and in the 32 jurisdictions opting for the "bubble concept," but one which was never waged in the Congress. Such policy arguments are more properly addressed to legislators or administrators, not to judges.[FN38]

> FN38. Respondents point out if a brand new factory that will emit over 100 tons of pollutants is constructed in a nonattainment area, that plant must obtain a permit pursuant to § 172(b)(6) and in order to do so, it must satisfy the § 173 conditions, including the LAER requirement. Respondents argue if an old plant containing several large emitting units is to be modernized by the replacement of one or more units emitting over 100 tons of pollutant with a new unit emitting less—but still more than 100 tons—the result should be no different simply because "it happens to be built not at a new site, but within a pre-existing plant." Brief for Respondents 4.

***865** In these cases, the Administrator's interpretation represents a reasonable accommodation of manifestly competing in ****2793** terests and is entitled to deference: the regulatory scheme is technical and complex, [FN39] the agency considered the matter in a detailed and reasoned fashion, [FN40] and the decision involves reconciling conflicting policies. [FN41] Congress intended to accommodate both interests, but did not do so itself on the level of specificity presented by these cases. Perhaps that body consciously desired the Administrator to strike the balance at this level, thinking that those with great expertise and charged with responsibility for administering the provision would be in a better position to do so; perhaps it simply did not consider the question at this level; and perhaps Congress was unable to forge a coalition on either side of the question, and those on each side decided to take their chances with the scheme devised by the agency. For judicial purposes, it matters not which of these things occurred.

FN39. See e.g., Aluminum Co. of America v. Central Lincoln Peoples' Util. Dist., 467 U.S., at 390, 104 S.Ct., at 2480 (1984).

FN40. See SEC v. Sloan, 436 U.S., at 117, 98 S.Ct., at 1711; Adamo Wrecking Co. v. United States, 434 U.S. 275, 287, n. 5, 98 S.Ct. 566, 574, n. 5, 54 L.Ed.2d 538 (1978); Skidmore v. Swift & Co., 323 U.S. 134, 140, 65 S.Ct. 161, 164, 89 L.Ed. 124 (1944).

FN41. See Capital Cities Cable, Inc. v. Crisp, 467 U.S. at 699–700, 104 S.Ct. at 2700–2701; United States v. Shimer, 367 U.S. 374, 382, 81 S.Ct. 1554, 1560, 6 L.Ed.2d 908 (1961).

Judges are not experts in the field, and are not part of either political branch of the Government. Courts must, in some cases, reconcile competing political interests, but not on the basis of the judges' personal policy preferences. In contrast, an agency to which Congress has delegated policy-making responsibilities may, within the limits of that delegation, properly rely upon the incumbent administration's views of wise policy to inform its judgments. While agencies are not directly accountable to the people, the Chief Executive is, and it is entirely appropriate for this political branch of the Government to make such policy choices—resolving the competing interests which Congress itself either inadvertently did not resolve, or intentionally left to be resolved by the ***866** agency charged with the administration of the statute in light of everyday realities.

When a challenge to an agency construction of a statutory provision, fairly conceptualized, really centers on the wisdom of the agency's policy, rather than whether it is a reasonable choice within a gap left open by Congress, the challenge must fail. In such a case, federal judges—who have no constituency—have a duty to respect legitimate policy choices made by those who do. The responsibilities for assessing the wisdom of such policy choices and resolving the struggle between competing views of the public interest are not judicial ones: "Our Constitution vests such responsibilities in the political branches." TVA v. Hill, 437 U.S. 153, 195, 98 S.Ct. 2279, 2302, 57 L.Ed.2d 117 (1978).

We hold that the EPA's definition of the term "source" is a permissible construction of the statute which seeks to accommodate progress in reducing air pollution with economic growth. "The Regulations which the Administrator has adopted provide what the agency could allowably view as ... [an] effective reconciliation of these twofold ends...." United States v. Shimer, 367 U.S., at 383, 81 S.Ct., at 1560.

The judgment of the Court of Appeals is reversed.

It is so ordered.

Justice MARSHALL and Justice REHNQUIST took no part in the consideration or decision of these cases.
Justice O'CONNOR took no part in the decision of these cases.

U.S.,1984
Chevron, U.S.A., Inc. v. Natural Resources Defense Council, Inc.
467 U.S. 837, 104 S.Ct. 2778, 21 ERC 1049, 81 L.Ed.2d 694, 14 Envtl. L. Rep. 20,507

END OF DOCUMENT

ASPATORE